Alex Pettes
July 2009

The Compassionate Life

The Compassionate Life

Tenzin Gyatso
THE FOURTEENTH DALAI LAMA

Wisdom Publications • Boston

Wisdom Publications, Inc.
199 Elm Street, Somerville MA 02144 USA
www.wisdompubs.org

Verses from the *Guide to the Bodhisattva's Way of Life* are adapted from the translation by Stephen Batchelor (Library of Tibetan Works and Archives, 1979). The translation of *Eight Verses for Training the Mind* is courtesy of John D. Dunne.

Library of Congress Cataloging-in-Publication Data
Bstan-'dzin-rgya-mtsho, Dalai Lama XIV, 1935–
    The compassionate life / Tenzin Gyatso.
      p. cm.
    Includes index.
    ISBN 0-86171-378-8 (alk. paper)
     1. Compassion—Religious aspects—Buddhism.
    2. Religious life—Buddhism. I. Title.
    BQ4360.B75 2001
    294.3'5677—dc21   2001026867

07   6 5 4

Cover design by Elizabeth Lawrence. Interior design by Gopa & Ted2.
Interior photos by Ueli Minder.

Wisdom Publications' books are printed on acid-free paper and meet the guidelines for permanence and durability set by the Committee on Production Guidelines for Book Longevity of the Council on Library Resources.

Printed in the United States of America.

Table of Contents

Publisher's Acknowledgment

THE PUBLISHER gratefully acknowledges the generous help of Richard Gere and the Gere Foundation in sponsoring the publication of this book.

Editor's Preface

IN HIS NUMEROUS PUBLIC APPEARANCES, His Holiness the Dalai Lama always returns to the topic of compassion. Compassion, or the desire to remove the suffering of another, is of course a central ideal for the practicing Buddhist. But one does not need to spend much time observing His Holiness to realize that his commitment to this virtue goes far beyond mere religious obligation. In his simple yet inimitable way, the Dalai Lama displays a profound recognition of the power of human affection in addressing the world's most urgent and complex problems.

At first glance, the Dalai Lama's rhetoric may seem almost naive, uninformed by a grasp of real-world politics and the subtleties of the human heart. Upon deeper inspection, however, it becomes clear that His Holiness speaks from a deep well of experience, grounded in his systematic training as a Buddhist monk and his personal experiences as the political and religious leader of the Tibetan people. His compassion is not timid or vague; it is solid, resolute, and above all wise. The difference is that His Holiness understands the mind—the power of our thoughts and emotions in shaping reality. He sees the precise relationship between the motivation we have and the results we get, and his life exemplifies the depth of his recognition.

It is our hope at Wisdom Publications that the teachings we have woven together to make this book will help advance His Holiness' own goals for world peace, religious tolerance, and spiritual development, while providing effective tools for those interested in cultivating lives of greater compassion.

David Kittelstrom

The Compassionate Life

The Benefits of Compassion

MY EXPERIENCES are nothing special, just ordinary human ones. Through my Buddhist training, however, I have learned something about compassion and developing a good heart, and that experience has proved very helpful in my day-to-day life. For example, the region of Tibet I come from is called Amdo, and people usually regard people who come from Amdo as short-tempered. So in Tibet, when someone would lose his or her temper, people would often take it as a sign that the person was from Amdo! However, when I compare my temperament now to the way it was when I was between the ages of fifteen and twenty, I see a noticeable difference. These days, I hardly find myself being irritated at all, and even when I am, it doesn't last long. This is a marvelous benefit of my own practice and training—now I am always quite cheerful!

In my lifetime, I have lost my country and have been reduced to being totally dependent on the goodwill of others. I have also lost my mother, and most of my tutors and lamas have passed away. Of course, these are tragic incidents, and I feel sad when I think about them. However, I don't feel overwhelmed by sadness. Old, familiar faces disappear and new faces appear, but I still maintain my happiness and peace of mind. This capacity to relate to events from a broader perspective is, for me, one of the marvels of human nature, and I believe it is rooted in our capacity for compassion and kindness toward others.

❧ OUR FUNDAMENTAL NATURE

Some of my friends have told me that while love and compassion are marvelous and good, they are not really very relevant. Our world, they say, is not a place where such virtues have much influence or power. They claim that anger and hatred are so much a part of human nature that humanity will always be dominated by them. I do not agree.

We humans have existed in our present form for about a hundred thousand years. I believe that if during this time the human mind had been primarily controlled by anger and hatred, our population would have decreased. But today, despite all our wars, we find that the human population is greater than ever. This clearly indicates to me that while anger and aggression are surely present, love and compassion predominate in the world. This is why what we call "news" is composed of mostly unpleasant or tragic events; compassionate activities are so much a part of daily life that they are taken for granted and therefore are largely ignored.

If we look at basic human nature, we can see that it is more gentle than aggressive. For example, if we examine various animals, we notice that animals of a more peaceful nature have a corresponding body structure, whereas predatory animals have a body structure that has developed according to their nature. Compare the tiger and the deer: there are great differences in their physical structures. When we compare our own body structure to theirs, we see that we resemble deer and rabbits more than tigers. Even our teeth are more like a rabbit's, are they not? They are not like a tiger's. Our fingernails are another good example—I cannot even harm a rat with a swipe of my fingernails alone. Of course, because of human intelligence, we are able to devise and use various tools and methods to accomplish things that would be difficult to accomplish without them. But because of our physical situation we belong to the gentle-animal category.

We are, after all, social animals. Without human friendship, without the human smile, our lives become miserable. The loneliness becomes unbearable. Such human interdependence is a natural law— that is to say, according to natural law, we depend on others to live.

If, under certain circumstances, because something is wrong inside us, our attitude toward our fellow human beings on whom we depend becomes hostile, how can we hope to attain peace of mind or a happy life? According to basic human nature or natural law, interdependence—giving and receiving affection—is the key to happiness.

This fact may become more evident if we reflect on the basic pattern of our existence. In order to do more than just barely survive, we need shelter, food, companions, friends, the esteem of others, resources, and so on; these things do not come about from ourselves alone but are all dependent on others. Suppose one single person were to live alone in a remote and uninhabited place. No matter how strong, healthy, or educated this person were, there would be no possibility of his or her leading a happy and fulfilling existence. If a person is living, for example, somewhere deep in the African jungle and is the only human being in an animal sanctuary, given that person's intelligence and cunning, the best he or she can do is to become, perhaps, king of the jungle. Can such a person have friends? Acquire renown? Can this person become a hero if he or she wishes to become one? I think the answer to all these questions is a definite no, for all these factors come about only in relation to other fellow humans.

When you are young, healthy, and strong, you sometimes can get the feeling that you are totally independent and do not need anyone else. But this is an illusion. Even at that prime age of your life, simply because your are a human being, you need friends, don't you? This is especially true when we become old. For example, in my own case, the Dalai Lama, who is now in his sixties, is beginning to show various signs of approaching old age. I can see the appearance of more white hair on my head, and I am also starting to experience problems sometimes with the knees when getting up or sitting down. As we grow old, we need to rely more and more on the help of others: this is the nature of our lives as human beings.

In at least one sense, we can say that other people are really the principal source of all our experiences of joy, happiness, and prosperity, and not only in terms of our day-to-day dealings with people. We can see that all the desirable experiences that we cherish or aspire to attain are dependent upon cooperation and interaction with others. It is an obvious fact. Similarly, from the point of view of a Buddhist practitioner, many of the high levels of realization that you gain and the progress that you make on your spiritual journey are dependent upon cooperation and interaction with others. Furthermore, at the stage of complete enlightenment, the compassionate activities of a buddha can come about spontaneously only in relation to other beings, for those beings are the recipients and beneficiaries of those enlightened activities.

Even from a totally selfish perspective—wanting only our own happiness, comfort, and satisfaction in life, with no consideration of others' welfare—I would still argue that the fulfillment of our aspirations depends upon others. Even the committing of harmful actions depends on the existence of others. For example, in order to cheat, you need someone as the object of your act.

All events and incidents in life are so intimately linked with the fate of others that a single person on his or her own cannot even begin to act. Many ordinary human activities, both positive and negative, cannot even be conceived of apart from the existence of other people. Because of others, we have the opportunity to earn money if that is what we desire in life. Similarly, in reliance upon the existence of others it becomes possible for the media to create fame or disrepute for someone. On your own you cannot create any fame or disrepute no matter how loud you might shout. The closest you can get is to create an echo of your own voice.

Thus interdependence is a fundamental law of nature. Not only higher forms of life but also many of the smallest insects are social beings who, without any religion, law, or education, survive by mutual cooperation based on an innate recognition of their interconnectedness. The most subtle level of material phenomena is also governed by interdependence. All phenomena, from the planet we inhabit to the oceans, clouds, forests, and flowers that surround us, arise in dependence upon subtle patterns of energy. Without their proper interaction, they dissolve and decay.

❧ Our Need for Love

One great question underlies our experience, whether we think about it consciously or not: What is the purpose of life? I believe that our life's purpose is to be happy. From the moment of birth, every human being wants happiness and does not want suffering. Neither social conditioning, nor education, nor ideology affect this. From the very core of our being, we simply desire contentment. I don't know whether the universe, with its countless galaxies, stars, and planets, has a deeper meaning or not, but at the very least, it is clear that we humans who live on this earth face the task of making a happy life for ourselves.

We are not like machine-made objects. We are more than just matter; we have feelings and experiences. If we were merely mechanical entities, then machines themselves could alleviate all of our suffering and fulfill all our needs. But material comfort alone is not enough. No material object, however beautiful or valuable, can make us feel loved. We need something deeper, what I usually refer to as human affection. With human affection, or compassion, all the material advantages that we have at our disposal can be very constructive and can produce good results. Without human affection, however, material advantages alone will not satisfy us, nor will they produce in us any measure of mental peace or happiness. In fact, material advantages without human affection may even create additional problems. So when we consider our origins and our nature we discover that no one is born free from the need for love. And although some modern schools of thought seek to do so, human beings cannot be defined as solely physical.

Ultimately, the reason why love and compassion bring the greatest happiness is simply that our nature cherishes them above all else. However capable and skillful an individual may be, left alone, he or she will not survive. However vigorous and independent we may feel during the most prosperous periods of life, when we are sick, or very young or very old, we depend on the support of others. Let's look more closely at the ways that affection and compassion help us throughout our lives.

Our beliefs may differ when it comes to questions of the creation and evolution of our universe, but we can at least agree that each of us is the product of our own parents. In general, our conception took place not just in the context of sexual desire but also from our parents' decision to have a child. Such decisions are founded on responsibility and altruism—the parents' compassionate commitment to care for their child until it is able to take care of itself. Thus, from the very moment of our conception, our parents' love is directly involved in our creation.

I learned from meeting with some scientists, especially those working in the field of neurobiology, that there is strong scientific evidence to suggest that even in pregnancy a mother's state of mind, be it calm or agitated, has a great effect on the physical and mental well-being of the unborn child. It seems vital for the mother to maintain a calm and relaxed state of mind. After birth, the first few weeks are the most crucial period for the healthy development of the child. During this time, I was told, one of the most important factors for ensuring rapid and healthy growth of the baby's brain is the mother's constant physical touch. If the child is left unattended and uncared for during this critical period, although the effects on the child's mental well being may not be immediately obvious, physical damage can result from this that will later become quite noticeable.

The central importance of love and caring continues throughout childhood. When a child sees someone with an open and affectionate demeanor, someone who is smiling or has a loving and caring expression, the child naturally feels happy and protected. On the other hand, if someone tries to hurt the child, it becomes gripped by fear, which leads to harmful consequences in terms of the child's development. Nowadays, many children grow up in unhappy homes. If they do not receive proper affection, in later life they will rarely love their parents and, not infrequently, will find it hard to love others. This is of course very sad.

As children grow older and enter school, their need for support must be met by their teachers. If a teacher not only imparts academic education but also assumes responsibility for preparing students for life, his or her pupils will feel trust and respect, and what has been taught will leave an indelible impression on their minds. On the other hand, subjects taught by a teacher who does not show true concern for students' overall well-being will be regarded as temporary and will not be retained for long.

Similarly, if one is sick and being treated in hospital by a doctor who evinces a warm human feeling, one feels at ease, and the doctor's desire to give the best possible care is itself curative, irrespective of the degree of his or her technical skill. On the other hand, if one's doctor lacks human feeling and displays an unfriendly expression, impatience, or casual disregard, one will feel anxious, even if the person is the most highly qualified doctor and the disease has been correctly diagnosed and the right medication prescribed. Inevitably, patients' feelings make a difference to the quality and completeness of their recovery.

Even in ordinary conversation in everyday life, when someone speaks with warm human feeling, we enjoy listening and respond accordingly; the whole conversation becomes interesting, however unimportant the topic may be. On the other hand, if a person speaks coldly or harshly, we feel uneasy and wish for a quick end to the interaction. From the least important to the most important event, the affection and respect of others are vital for our happiness.

Recently I met another group of scientists in America who said that the rate of mental illness in their country was quite high, around 12 percent of the population. It became clear during our discussion that depression was caused not by a lack of material necessities but more likely by a difficulty in giving and receiving affection.

So, as you can see from all of this, whether or not we are consciously aware of it, from the day we are born, the need for human affection is in our very blood. Even if the affection comes from an animal or someone we would normally consider an enemy, both children and adults will naturally gravitate toward it.

❧ THE ULTIMATE SOURCE OF SUCCESS

As human beings we all have the potential to be happy and compassionate people, and we also have the potential to be miserable and harmful to others. The potential for all these things is present within each of us. If we want to be happy, then the important thing is to try to promote the positive and useful aspects in each of us and to try to reduce the negative. Doing negative things, such as stealing and lying, may occasionally seem to bring some short-term satisfaction, but in the long term they will always bring us misery. Positive acts always bring us inner strength. With inner strength we have less fear and more self-confidence, and it becomes much easier to extend our sense of caring to others without any barriers, whether religious, cultural, or otherwise. It is thus very important to recognize our potential for both good and bad, and then to observe and analyze it carefully.

This is what I call the promotion of human value. My main concern is always how to promote an understanding of deeper human value. This deeper human value is compassion, a sense of caring, and commitment. No matter what your religion, and whether you are a believer or a nonbeliever, without them you cannot be happy.

Let's examine the usefulness of compassion and a good heart in daily life. If we are in a good mood when we get up in the morning, if there is a warm-hearted feeling within, automatically our inner door is opened for that day. Even should an unfriendly person happen along, we would not experience much disturbance and might even manage to say something nice to that person. We could chat with the not-so-friendly person and perhaps even have a meaningful conversation. Once we create a friendly and positive atmosphere, it automatically helps to reduce fear and insecurity. In this way we can easily make more friends and create more smiles.

But on a day when our mood is less positive and we are feeling irritated, automatically our inner door closes. As a result, even if we encounter our best friend, we feel uncomfortable and strained. These instances show how our inner attitude makes a great difference in our

daily experiences. In order to create a pleasant atmosphere within ourselves, within our families, within our communities, we have to realize that the ultimate source of that pleasant atmosphere is within the
individual, within each of us—a good heart, human compassion, love.

Compassion doesn't have only mental benefits, but it contributes to good physical health as well. According to contemporary
medicine, as well as to my personal experience, mental stability
and physical well-being are directly related. Without question, anger
and agitation make us more susceptible to illness. On the other
hand, if the mind is tranquil and occupied with positive thoughts,
the body will not easily fall prey to disease. This shows that the
physical body itself appreciates and responds to human affection,
human peace of mind.

Another thing that is quite clear to me is that the moment you
think only of yourself, the focus of your whole reality narrows, and
because of this narrow focus, uncomfortable things can appear huge
and bring you fear and discomfort and a sense of feeling overwhelmed by misery. The moment you think of others with a sense of
caring, however, your view widens. Within that wider perspective,
your own problems appear to be of little significance, and this makes
a big difference.

If you have a sense of caring for others, you will manifest a kind
of inner strength in spite of your own difficulties and problems. With

this strength, your own problems will seem less significant and bothersome to you. By going beyond your own problems and taking care of others, you gain inner strength, self-confidence, courage, and a greater sense of calm. This is a clear example of how one's way of thinking can really make a difference.

One's own self-interest and wishes are fulfilled as a byproduct of actually working for other sentient beings. As the well-known fifteenth-century master Tsongkhapa points out in his *Great Exposition of the Path to Enlightenment,* "The more the practitioner engages in activities and thoughts that are focused and directed toward the fulfillment of others' well-being, the fulfillment or realization of his or her own aspiration will come as a byproduct without having to make a separate effort." Some of you may have actually heard me remark, which I do quite often, that in some sense the bodhisattvas, the compassionate practitioners of the Buddhist path, are "wisely selfish" people, whereas people like us are the "foolishly selfish." We think of ourselves and disregard others, and the result is that we always remain unhappy and have a miserable time.

Other benefits of altruism and a good heart may not be so obvious to us. One aim of Buddhist practice is to achieve a favorable birth in our next life, a goal that can be attained only by restraining from actions that are harmful to others. Therefore, even in the context of such an aim, we find that altruism and a good heart are at the root. It is also very clear that for a bodhisattva to be successful in accomplishing the practice of the six perfections—of generosity, ethical discipline, tolerance, joyous effort, concentration, and wisdom—cooperation with and kindness toward fellow beings are extremely important.

Thus we find that kindness and a good heart form the underlying foundation for our success in this life, our progress on the spiritual path, and our fulfillment of our ultimate aspiration, the attainment of full enlightenment. Hence, compassion and a good heart are not only important at the beginning but also in the middle and at the end. Their necessity and value are not limited to any specific time, place, society, or culture.

Thus, we not only need compassion and human affection to survive, but they are the ultimate sources of success in life. Selfish ways of thinking not only harm others, they prevent the very happiness we ourselves desire. The time has come to think more wisely, hasn't it? This is my belief.

2

Developing Compassion

BEFORE WE CAN GENERATE COMPASSION and love, it is important to have a clear understanding of what we understand compassion and love to be. In simple terms, compassion and love can be defined as positive thoughts and feelings that give rise to such essential things in life as hope, courage, determination, and inner strength. In the Buddhist tradition, compassion and love are seen as two aspects of same thing: Compassion is the wish for another being to be free from suffering; love is wanting them to have happiness.

The next matter to be understood is whether it is possible to enhance compassion and love. In other words, is there a means by which these qualities of mind can be increased and anger, hatred, and jealousy reduced? My answer to this is an emphatic, "Yes!" Even if you do not agree with me right now, let yourself be open to the possibility of such development. Let us carry out some experiments together; perhaps we may then find some answers.

For a start, it is possible to divide every kind of happiness and suffering into two main categories: mental and physical. Of the two, it is the mind that exerts the greatest influence on most of us. Unless we are either gravely ill or deprived of basic necessities, our physical condition plays a secondary role in life. If the body is content, we virtually ignore it. The mind, however, registers every event, no matter how small. Hence we should devote our most serious efforts to bringing about mental peace rather than physical comfort.

❧ THE MIND CAN BE CHANGED

From my own limited experience, I am convinced that through constant training we can indeed develop our minds. Our positive attitudes, thoughts, and outlook can be enhanced, and their negative counterparts can be reduced. Even a single moment of consciousness depends on so many factors, and when we change these various factors, the mind also changes. This is a simple truth about the nature of mind.

The thing that we call "mind" is quite peculiar. Sometimes it is very stubborn and very resistant to change. With continuous effort, however, and with conviction based on reason, our minds are sometimes quite honest and flexible. When we truly recognize that there is some need to change, then our minds can change. Wishing and praying alone will not transform your mind; you also need reason— reason ultimately grounded in your own experience. And you won't be able to transform your mind overnight; old habits, especially mental ones, resist quick solutions. But with effort over time and conviction grounded in reason, you can definitely achieve profound changes in your mental attitudes.

As a basis for change, we need to recognize that as long as we live in this world we will encounter problems, things that obstruct the fulfillment of our goals. If, when these happen, we lose hope and become discouraged, we diminish our ability to face these difficulties. If, on the other hand, we remember that not just we but everyone has to undergo suffering, this more realistic perspective will increase our determination and our capacity to overcome troubles. By remembering the suffering of others, by feeling compassion for others, our own suffering becomes manageable. Indeed, with this attitude, each new obstacle can be seen as yet another valuable opportunity to improve our mind, another opportunity for deepening our compassion! With each new experience, we can strive gradually to become more compassionate; that is, we can develop both genuine sympathy for others' suffering and the will to help remove their pain. As a result, our own serenity and inner strength will increase.

❧ How to Develop Compassion

Self-centeredness inhibits our love for others, and we are all afflicted by it to one degree or another. For true happiness to come about, we need a calm mind, and such peace of mind is brought about only by a compassionate attitude. How can we develop this attitude? Obviously, it is not enough for us simply to believe that compassion is important and to think about how nice it is! We need to make a concerted effort to develop it; we must use all the events of our daily life to transform our thoughts and behavior.

First of all, we must be clear about what we mean by *compassion*. Many forms of compassionate feeling are mixed with desire and attachment. For instance, the love parents feel for their child is often strongly associated with their own emotional needs, so it is not fully compassionate. Usually when we are concerned about a close friend, we call this compassion, but it too is usually attachment. Even in marriage, the love between husband and wife—particularly at the beginning, when each partner still may not know the other's deeper character very well—depends more on attachment than genuine love. Marriages that last only a short time do so because they lack compassion; they are produced by emotional attachment based on projection and expectation, and as soon as the projections change, the attachment disappears. Our desire can be so strong that the person to whom we are attached appears flawless, when in fact he or she has many faults. In addition, attachment makes us exaggerate small, positive qualities. When this happens, it indicates that our love is motivated more by personal need than by genuine care for another.

Compassion without attachment is possible. Therefore, we need to clarify the distinctions between compassion and attachment. True compassion is not just an emotional response but a firm commitment founded on reason. Because of this firm foundation, a truly compassionate attitude toward others does not change even if they behave negatively. Genuine compassion is based not on our own projections and expectations, but rather on the needs of the other: irrespective of whether another person is a close friend or an enemy, as long as that person wishes for peace and happiness and wishes to overcome suffering, then on that basis we develop genuine concern for their problem. This is genuine compassion. For a Buddhist practitioner, the goal is to develop this genuine compassion, this genuine wish for the well-being of another, in fact for every living being throughout the universe. Of course, developing this kind of compassion is not at all easy! Let us consider this point more closely.

Whether people are beautiful or plain, friendly or cruel, ultimately they are human beings, just like oneself. Like oneself, they want happiness and do not want suffering. Furthermore, their right to overcome suffering and to be happy is equal to one's own. Now, when you recognize that all beings are equal in both their desire for happiness and their right to obtain it, you automatically feel empathy and closeness for them. Through accustoming your mind to this sense of universal altruism, you develop a feeling of responsibility for others; you wish to help them actively overcome their problems. This wish is not selective; it applies equally to all beings. As long as they experience pleasure and pain just as you do, there is no logical basis to discriminate between them or to alter your concern for them if they behave negatively.

One point I should make here is that some people, especially those who see themselves as very realistic and practical, are sometimes *too* realistic and obsessed with practicality. They may think, "The idea of wishing for the happiness of all beings, of wanting what is best for every single one, is unrealistic and too idealistic. Such an unrealistic idea cannot contribute in any way to transforming the mind or to attaining some kind of mental discipline, because it is completely unachievable."

A more effective approach, they may think, would be to begin with a close circle of people with whom one has direct interaction. Later one can expand and increase the parameters of that circle. They feel there is simply no point in thinking about all beings since there is an infinite number of them. They may conceivably be able to feel some kind of connection with some fellow human beings on this planet, but they feel that the infinite number of beings throughout the universe have nothing to do with their own experience as individuals. They may ask, "What point is there in trying to cultivate the mind that tries to include within its sphere every living being?"

In other contexts, that might be a valid objection. What is important here, however, is to grasp the impact of cultivating such altruistic sentiments. The point is to try to develop the scope of our empathy in such a way that we can extend it to any form of life with the capacity to feel pain and experience happiness. It is a matter of recognizing living organisms as sentient, and therefore subject to pain and capable of happiness.

Such a universal sentiment of compassion is very powerful, and there is no need to be able to identify, in specific terms, with every single living being in order for it to be effective. In this regard it is similar to recognizing the universal nature of impermanence: when we cultivate the recognition that all things and events are impermanent, we do not need to consider individually every single thing that exists in the universe in order to be convinced of it. That is not how the mind works. It is important to appreciate this point.

Given patience and time, it is within our power to develop this kind of universal compassion. Of course our self-centeredness, our distinctive attachment to the feeling of a solid "I," works fundamentally to inhibit our compassion. Indeed, true compassion can be experienced only when this type of self-grasping is eliminated. But this does not mean that we cannot start to cultivate compassion and begin to make progress right away.

❧ How We Can Start

We should begin by removing the greatest hindrances to compassion: anger and hatred. As we all know, these extremely powerful emotions can overwhelm our minds. Nevertheless, despite their power, anger and hatred can be controlled. If we don't control them, these negative emotions will plague us—with no extra effort on their part!— and impede our quest for the happiness of a loving mind.

You may not feel that anger is a hindrance, so, as a start, it is useful to investigate whether anger is of value. Sometimes, when we are discouraged by a difficult situation, anger does seem helpful, appearing to bring with it more energy, confidence, and determination. In these moments, though, we must examine our mental state carefully. While it is true that anger brings extra energy, if we explore the nature of this energy, we discover that it is blind: we cannot be sure whether its result will be positive or negative. This is because anger eclipses the best part of our brain: its rationality. So the energy of anger is almost always unreliable. It can cause an immense amount of destructive, unfortunate behavior. Moreover, if anger increases to the extreme, one becomes a crazy person, acting in ways that are as damaging to oneself as they are to others.

It is possible, however, to develop an equally forceful but far more controlled energy with which to handle difficult situations. This controlled energy comes not only from a compassionate attitude, but also from reason and patience. These are the most powerful antidotes to anger. Unfortunately, many people misjudge reason and patience as signs of weakness. I believe the opposite to be true: that they are the true signs of inner strength. Compassion is by nature gentle, peaceful, and soft, but it is also very powerful. It gives us inner strength and allows us to be patient. It is those who easily lose their patience who are insecure and unstable. Thus, to me, the arousal of anger is usually a direct sign of weakness.

So, when a problem first arises, try to remain humble and maintain a sincere attitude and be concerned that the outcome will be fair. Of course, others may try to take advantage of your concern for fairness, and if your remaining detached only encourages unjust aggression, adopt a strong stand. This should be done with compassion, however, and if it becomes necessary to express your views and take strong countermeasures, do so without anger or ill intent.

You should realize that even though your opponents appear to be harming you, in the end, their destructive activity will damage only themselves. In order to check your own selfish impulse to retaliate, you should recall your desire to practice compassion and assume responsibility for helping prevent the other person from suffering the consequences of their acts. If the measures you employ have been calmly chosen, they will be more effective, more accurate, and more forceful. Retaliation based on the blind energy of anger seldom hits the target.

❧ FRIENDS AND ENEMIES

I must emphasize again that merely thinking that compassion and reason and patience are good will not be enough to develop them. We must wait for difficulties to arise and then attempt to practice them. And who creates such opportunities? Not our friends, of course, but our enemies. They are the ones who give us the most trouble. So if we truly wish to learn, we should consider enemies our best teachers! For a person who cherishes compassion and love, the practice of patience is essential, and for that, enemies are indispensable. So we should feel grateful to our enemies, for it is they who can best help us develop a tranquil mind! Furthermore, it is often the case in both personal and public life that with a change in circumstances, enemies become friends.

Of course, it is natural and right that we all want friends. But is friendship produced through quarrels and anger, jealousy and intense competitiveness? I do not think so. The best way to make friends is to be very compassionate! Only affection brings us genuine close friends. You should take good care of others, be concerned for their welfare, help them, serve them, make more friends, make more smiles. The result? When you yourself need help, you'll find plenty of helpers! If, on the other hand, you neglect the happiness of others, in the long term you will be the loser.

In today's materialistic society, if you have money and power you may seem to have many friends. But they are not friends of yours; they are friends of your money and power. When you lose your wealth and influence, you will find it very difficult to track these people down.

The trouble is that when things in the world go well for us, we become confident that we can manage by ourselves and feel we do not need friends, but as our status or health declines, we quickly realize how wrong we were. So to prepare for that time, to make genuine friends who will help us when the need arises, we ourselves must cultivate compassion!

Though sometimes people laugh when I say it, I myself always want more friends. I love smiles. Because of this I have the problem of knowing how to make more friends and how to get more smiles, in particular, genuine smiles. There are other kinds of smiles, such as sarcastic, artificial, or diplomatic smiles. Many smiles produce no feeling of satisfaction, and sometimes they can even create suspicion or fear, can't they? But a genuine smile really gives us a feeling of freshness and is, I believe, unique to human beings. If these are the smiles we want, then we ourselves must create the reasons for them to appear.

So how do we make friends? Certainly not through hatred and confrontation. It is impossible to make friends by hitting people and fighting with them. A genuine friendship can emerge only through cooperation based on honesty and sincerity, and this means having an open mind and a warm heart. This, I think, is obvious from our own everyday interactions with others.

❧ OVERCOMING THE ENEMY WITHIN

Anger and hatred are our real enemies. They are the forces we most need to confront and defeat, not the temporary "enemies" who appear intermittently throughout our life. And unless we train our minds to reduce their negative force, they will continue to disturb us and disrupt our attempts to develop a calm mind.

To eliminate the destructive potential of anger and hatred entirely, we need to recognize that the root of anger lies in the attitude that cherishes our own welfare and benefit while remaining oblivious to the well-being of others. This self-centered attitude underlies not only anger, but virtually all our states of mind. It is a deluded attitude, mis-perceiving the way things actually are, and this misperception is responsible for all the suffering and dissatisfaction that we experience. Therefore, the first task of a practitioner of compassion and a good heart is to gain an understanding of the destructive nature of this inner enemy and of how it naturally and inevitably leads to undesirable con-sequences.

In order to see this destructive process clearly, we need to become aware of the nature of the mind. I always tell people that the mind is a very complex phenomenon. According to Buddhist philosophy, there are many types of mind, or consciousness, and in Buddhist meditation we develop a deep familiarity with our ever-changing mental states.

In scientific research, we analyze matter in terms of its con-stituent particles. We actualize the potential of the various molecular and chemical compositions and atomic structures that have beneficial value, while we neglect, or in some cases deliberately eliminate, those that lack such useful properties. This discriminatory approach has led to some fascinating results.

If we paid a similar amount of attention to analyzing our mind, the world of experience and mental phenomena, we would discov-er that there are multitudes of mental states, differing in their modes of apprehension, object, degree of intensity of engagement with their object, and so on. Certain aspects of mind are useful and beneficial, so we should correctly identify them and enhance their potential. Like scientists, if we discover upon examination that certain states of mind are unwholesome in that they bring us suffering and problems, then we should seek a way to eradicate them. This is indeed a most worthwhile project. In fact, this is the greatest concern for Buddhist practitioners. It is quite similar to opening one's skull to carry out experiments on those tiny cells with the aim of determining which cells bring us joy and which cells cause disturbances. As long as these inner enemies remain secure within, there is great danger.

When approaching a technique like the Buddhist training of the mind, we must understand and appreciate the complexity of the task we are facing. Buddhist scriptures mention eighty-four thousand types of negative and destructive thoughts, which have eighty-four thousand corresponding approaches or antidotes. It is important not to have the unrealistic expectation that somehow, somewhere, we will find a single magic key that will help us eradicate all of these negativities. We need to apply many different methods over a long period of time in order to bring lasting results. Therefore, we need great determination and patience. It is wrong to expect that once you start Dharma practice, you'll become enlightened within a short period of time, perhaps in one week. This is unrealistic.

The famous Buddhist saint Nagarjuna wrote beautifully about the need for patience and an appreciation for the length of time that is required to really engage in a process of mental training. Nagarjuna said that if—through mental training and discipline, through insight and its skillful application—you can develop within yourself a sense of ease and confidence, an ease that is rooted in a confirmed definitive stance, the time that it takes to become enlightened does not matter. In contrast to Nagarjuna, in our own personal experience, time *does* matter. If we are experiencing an unbearably miserable event, even for a short time, we feel impatient. We want to get out of the state as soon as possible.

Since compassion and a good heart are developed through constant and conscious effort, it is important for us first to identify the favorable conditions that give rise to our own qualities of kindness and then to identify the adverse circumstances that obstruct our cultivation of these positive states of mind. It is therefore important for us to lead a life of constant mindfulness and mental alertness. Our mastery of mindfulness should be such that whenever a new situation arises, we are able to immediately recognize whether the circumstances are favorable or adverse to the development of compassion and a good heart. By pursuing the practice of compassion in such a manner, we will gradually be able to alleviate the effects of the obstructive forces and enhance the conditions that favor the development of compassion and a good heart.

As I mentioned earlier, every kind of happiness and suffering is primarily either physical or mental. When pain comes mainly in the form of physical sensations, it can be alleviated by a positive mental state; if your mental state is calm, this can neutralize the pain. An attitude of acceptance or willingness to endure that physical pain can also make a big difference. On the other hand, if your pain is primarily mental and not physical, then it is very difficult to get any relief from physical comfort. You may attempt to neutralize the pain through sensory gratification, but that never succeeds for long and may in fact make your pain worse. Therefore, it is very useful and important to concentrate on mental training on a daily basis, even apart from spiritual considerations of the time of death or the path to enlightenment. Even for those who are not interested in such long-term concerns, it is more worthwhile to take care of our mind than to only take care of our money.

Of course Buddhism is concerned not only with relieving one's own pain, but with securing the freedom from suffering for all living beings. Yet if it is so difficult to bear our own pain, how can we even conceive of taking on the responsibility for the suffering of all beings? In his great work, *Guide to the Bodhisattva's Way of Life,* the eighth-century Indian master Shantideva says that there is a phenomenological difference between the pain that you experience when you take someone else's pain upon yourself and the pain that comes directly from your own pain and suffering. In the former, there is an element of discomfort because you are sharing the other's pain; however, there is also a certain amount of stability because, in a sense, you are voluntarily accepting that pain. In the voluntary participation in others' suffering there is strength and a sense of confidence. But in the latter case, when you are undergoing your own pain and suffering, there is an element of involuntariness, and because of that lack of control on your part, you feel weak and completely overwhelmed.

In the Buddhist teachings on altruism and compassion, certain expressions are used such as "Disregard your own well-being and cherish the well-being of others." Such exhortations may sound intimidating, but it is important to understand these statements regarding the practice of voluntarily sharing someone else's pain and suffering in their proper context. Fundamentally, the basis on which you can build a sense of caring for others is the capacity to love yourself.

Love for yourself does not arise from some great debt you owe yourself. Rather, the capacity to love yourself is based on the fact that we all naturally desire happiness and want to avoid suffering. And once you recognize this love in relation to yourself, then you can extend it to other sentient beings. Therefore, when you find statements in the teachings such as "Disregard your own well-being and cherish the well-being of others," you should understand them in the context of training yourself according to the ideal of compassion. This is important if we are not to indulge in self-centered ways of thinking that disregard the impact of our actions on others.

We can develop the attitude of considering other sentient beings as precious by recognizing the part their kindness plays in our own experience of joy, happiness, and success. This should be our first consideration. Next we should consider that, through analysis, we can see that much of our misery and pain result from a self-centered attitude that cherishes our own well-being at the expense of others, whereas much of the joy and sense of security in our lives arise from thoughts and emotions that cherish the well-being of others. Contrasting these two—cherishing ourselves alone versus cherishing others—convinces us of the need to regard others' well-being as precious.

❧ Equanimity

Because genuine compassion is universal and does not discriminate, cultivating compassion must first involve cultivating equanimity toward all sentient beings. For example, you may know that such-and-such a person is your friend or relative in this life, but Buddhism points out that this person may have been your worst enemy in a past life. You can apply the same sort of reasoning to someone you consider an enemy: although this person may behave negatively toward you and is your enemy in this life, he or she could have been your best friend or even your mother in a past life. By reflecting upon the fluctuating nature of one's relationships with others and also on the potential that exists in all sentient beings to be both friends and enemies, you can develop this even-mindedness or equanimity.

The practice of developing equanimity involves a form of detachment, but it is important to understand what *detachment* means. Sometimes when people hear about the Buddhist practice of detachment, they think that Buddhism is advocating indifference toward all things, but that is not the case. Cultivating detachment takes the sting out of our emotions toward others that are based on superficial considerations of distance or closeness. Then, on that basis, we can develop a compassion that is truly universal. Detachment does not mean indifference to the world or life—precisely the opposite. A profound experience of detachment is the ground on which we can build genuine compassion extending to all other sentient beings.

3
Global Compassion

I BELIEVE that at every level of society—familial, national, and international—the key to a happier and more successful world is the growth of compassion. We do not need to become religious, nor do we need to believe in a particular ideology. All that is necessary is for each of us to develop our good human qualities. I believe that the cultivation of individual happiness can contribute in a profound and effective way to the overall improvement of the entire human community.

We all share an identical need for love, and on the basis of this commonality, it is possible to feel that anybody we meet, in whatever circumstances, is a brother or sister. No matter how new the face or how different the dress or behavior, there is no significant division between us and other people. It is foolish to dwell on external differences because our basic natures are the same.

The benefits of transcending such superficial differences become clear when we look at our global situation. Ultimately humanity is one, and this small planet is our only home. If we are to protect this home of ours, each of us needs to experience a vivid sense of universal altruism and compassion. It is only this feeling that can remove the self-centered motives that cause people to deceive and misuse one another. If you have a sincere and open heart, you naturally feel self-worth and confidence, and there is no need to be fearful of others.

The need for an atmosphere of openness and cooperation at the global level is becoming more urgent. In this modern age, when it comes to dealing with economic situations, there are no longer familial or even national boundaries. From country to country and continent to continent, the world is inextricably interconnected. Each country depends heavily on the others. In order for a country to develop its own economy, it is forced to take seriously into account the economic conditions of other countries as well. In fact, economic improvement in other countries ultimately results in economic improvement in one's own country. In view of these facts about our modern world, we need a total revolution in our thinking and our habits. It is becoming clearer every day that a viable economic system must be based on a true sense of universal responsibility. In other words, what we need is a genuine commitment to the principles of universal brotherhood and sisterhood. This much is clear, isn't it? This is not just a holy, moral, or religious ideal. Rather, it is the reality of our modern human existence.

If you reflect deeply enough, it becomes obvious that we need more compassion and altruism everywhere. This critical point can be appreciated by observing the current state of affairs in the world, whether in the fields of modern economics and health care, or in political and military situations. In addition to the multitude of social and political crises, the world is also facing an ever-increasing cycle of natural calamities. Year after year, we have witnessed a radical shifting of global climatic patterns that has led to grave consequences: excessive rain in some countries that has brought serious flooding, a shortage of precipitation in other countries that has resulted in devastating droughts. Fortunately, concern for ecology and the environment is rapidly growing everywhere. We are now beginning to appreciate that the question of environmental protection is ultimately a question of our very survival on this planet. As human beings, we must also respect our fellow members of the human family: our neighbors, our friends, and so forth. Compassion, loving-kindness, altruism, and a sense of brotherhood and sisterhood are the keys not only to human development, but to planetary survival.

The success or failure of humanity in the future depends primarily upon the will and determination of the present generation. If we ourselves do not utilize our faculties of will and intelligence, there is no one else who can guarantee our future and that of the next generation. This is an indisputable fact. We cannot place the entire blame on politicians or those people who are seen as directly responsible for various situations; we too must bear some responsibility personally. It is only when the individual accepts personal responsibility that he or she begins to take some initiative. Just shouting and complaining is not good enough. A genuine change must first come from within the individual, then he or she can attempt to make significant contributions to humanity. Altruism is not merely a religious ideal; it is an indispensable requirement for humanity at large.

If we look at human history, we will find that a good heart has been the key in achieving what the world regards as great accomplishments: in the fields of civil rights, social work, political liberation, and religion, for example. A sincere outlook and motivation do not belong exclusively to the sphere of religion; they can be generated by anyone simply by having genuine concern for others, for one's community, for the poor and the needy. In short, they arise from taking a deep interest in and being concerned about the welfare of the larger community, that is, the welfare of others. Actions resulting from this kind of attitude and motivation will go down in history as good, beneficial, and a service to humanity. Today, when we read of such acts from history, although the events are in the past and have become only memories, we still feel happy and comforted because of them. We recall with a deep sense of admiration that this or that person did a great and noble work. We can also see a few examples of such greatness in our own generation.

On the other hand, our history also abounds with stories of individuals perpetrating the most destructive and harmful acts: killing and torturing other people, bringing misery and untold suffering to large numbers of human beings. These incidents can be seen to reflect the darker side of our common human heritage. Such events occur only when there is hatred, anger, jealousy, and unbounded greed. World history is simply the collective record of the effects of the negative and positive thoughts of human beings. This, I think, is quite clear. By reflecting on history, we can see that if we want to have a better and happier future, we must examine our mindset now and reflect on the way of life that this mindset will bring about in the future. The pervasive power of these negative attitudes cannot be overstated.

❧ COMPASSION AND CONFLICT RESOLUTION

Given our current global situation, cooperation is essential, especially in fields such as economics and education. The idea that international differences are paramount has been made less viable by the movement toward a unified Western Europe. This movement is, I think, truly marvelous and very timely. Yet this close work between nations did not come about because of compassion or religious faith, but rather through necessity. There is a growing tendency in the world toward global awareness. Under the current circumstances a closer relationship with others has become an element essential to our very survival. Therefore, the concept of universal responsibility based on compassion and on a sense of brotherhood and sisterhood is now essential. The world is full of conflicts—conflicts due to ideology, religion—even conflicts within families. These are all conflicts based on one person wanting one thing and another wanting something else. But if we try to find the cause of these many conflicts, we discover that there are in fact many different sources, many different causes, even within ourselves.

Yet even before we understand the causes of all our conflicts, we have the potential and ability to come together in harmony. All the causes are relative. Although there are many sources of conflict, there are at the same time many sources of unity and harmony. The time has come to put more emphasis on unity. Here again there must be human affection and patient analysis grounded in compassion.

For example, you may have a different ideological or religious opinion from someone else. If you respect the other's rights and sincerely show a compassionate attitude toward that person, then it does not matter whether their idea is suitable for you; that is secondary. As long as the other person believes in it and derives some benefits from such a viewpoint, it is his or her absolute right. So we must respect that and accept the fact that different viewpoints exist. In the realm of economics as well, one's competitors must also receive some profit, because they too have to survive. When we have a broader perspective based on compassion, I think things become much easier. Once again, compassion is the key factor.

❧ DEMILITARIZATION

In some regards, our world situation today has eased. The Cold War between the former Soviet Union and the United States is over. Instead of looking for new enemies, we should now think and talk seriously about global demilitarization, or at least the idea of demilitarization. I always tell my American friends, "Your strength comes not from nuclear weapons but from your ancestors' noble ideas of freedom, liberty, and democracy."

When I was in the United States in 1991, I had the opportunity of meeting with former President George Bush. At that time we discussed the New World Order, and I said to him, "A New World Order with compassion is very good. I'm not so sure about a New World Order without compassion."

I believe that the time has come to think and talk about demilitarization. With the breakup of the former Soviet Union, we saw some signs of weapons reduction and, for the first time, denuclearization. Step by step, I think our goal should be to free the world—our small planet—from weapons. This does not mean, however, that we should abolish all forms of weapons. We may need to keep some, since there are always some mischievous people and groups among us. In order to take precautions and be safeguarded from these sources, we could create a system of regionally monitored international police forces, not necessarily belonging to any one nation but controlled collectively and supervised ultimately by an organization like the United Nations or a similar international body. That way, with no weapons available to any individual nation, there would be no danger of military conflict between nations, and there would be no civil war.

War, sadly, has remained a part of human history up to the present, but I think the time has come to change the concepts that lead to war. Some people consider war to be something glorious; they think that through war they can become heroes. This attitude toward war is very wrong. Recently an interviewer remarked to me, "Westerners have a great fear of death, but Easterners seem to have very little fear of death."

To that I half-jokingly responded, "It seems to me that, to the Western mind, war and the military establishment are extremely important. War means death—by killing, not by natural causes. So it seems that, in fact, you are the ones who do not fear death, because you are so fond of war. We Easterners, particularly Tibetans, cannot even begin to consider war; we cannot conceive of fighting, because the inevitable result of war is disaster: death, injuries, and misery. Therefore, the concept of war, in our minds, is extremely negative. That would seem to mean we actually have more fear of death than you. Don't you think?"

Unfortunately, because of certain factors, people persist with incorrect ideas about war. The danger of these ideas for the world community is greater than ever, so we need to seriously consider demilitarization. I felt this very strongly during and after the Persian Gulf crisis. Of course, everybody blamed Saddam Hussein, and there is no question that Saddam Hussein was harmful—he made many mistakes and acted wrongly in many ways. After all, he is a dictator, and a dictator is, of course, something harmful. However, without his military establishment, without his weapons, Saddam Hussein could not function as that kind of dictator. Who supplied those weapons? The suppliers also bear the responsibility. Some Western nations supplied him with weapons without regard for the consequences.

To think only of money, of making a profit from selling weapons, is terrible. I once met a Frenchwoman who had spent many years in Beirut. She told me with great sadness that during the crisis in Beirut there were people at one end of the city making a profit selling weapons, and that every day, at the other end of the city, other—innocent—people were being killed with those very weapons. Similarly, on one side of our planet there are people living a lavish life with the profits made from selling arms, while innocent people are getting killed with those sophisticated arms on the other side of our planet. Therefore, the first step is to stop selling weapons. Sometimes I tease my Swedish friends: "Oh, you are really wonderful. During the last period of conflict you remained neutral. And you always consider the importance of human rights and world peace. Very good. But in the meantime you are selling many weapons. This is a little hypocritical, isn't it?"

At the time of the Persian Gulf crisis I made an inner pledge—a commitment that for the rest of my life I would contribute to furthering the idea of demilitarization. As far as my own country is concerned, I have made up my mind that in the future, Tibet should be a completely demilitarized zone. Once again, in working to bring about demilitarization, the key factor is human compassion.

4

Religious Pluralism

U NLESS WE KNOW the value of other religious traditions, it is difficult to develop respect for them. Mutual respect is the foundation of genuine harmony. We should strive for a spirit of harmony, not for political or economic reasons, but rather simply because we realize the value of other traditions. I always make an effort to promote religious harmony.

Drawing on religious faith to promote basic human values is something very positive. The major world religions all teach love, compassion, and forgiveness. The way each religious tradition promotes these is different, of course, but since they aim at more or less the same goals—having a happier life, becoming a more compassionate person, and creating a more compassionate world— their different methods do not present an inherent problem. The ultimate achievement of love, compassion, and forgiveness is what is important. All the major world religions have the same potential to help humanity. Some people have a disposition that is suited to religious faith, and because of the variety of dispositions among humans, it logically follows that we need different religions. The variety is beneficial. I'd like to address the topic of religious harmony by defining two levels of spirituality.

❧ THE FIRST LEVEL OF SPIRITUALITY: FAITH AND TOLERANCE

At the first level of spirituality, for human beings everywhere, is faith. This is true for each of the major world religions. I believe each of these religions has its own important role, but in order for them to make an effective contribution to the benefit of humanity, two important factors must be considered.

The first of these factors is that the individual practitioners of the various religions—that is, we ourselves—must practice sincerely. Religious teachings must be an integral part of our lives; they should not be separate from our lives. Sometimes we go into a church or temple and say a prayer or generate some kind of spiritual feeling, and then, when we step outside the church or temple, none of that religious feeling remains. This is not the proper way to practice. The religious message must be with us wherever we are. The teachings of our religion must be present in our lives so that, when we really need or require blessings or inner strength, those teachings and the effects of those teachings will be there for us. They will be there when we experience difficulties because they are constantly present.

Only when religion has become an integral part of our lives can it be really effective. We need to know these teachings not only on an intellectual level but also through our own deeper experience. Sometimes we understand different religious ideas on an overly superficial or intellectual level. Without a deeper feeling, the effectiveness of religion becomes limited. Therefore, we must practice sincerely, and integrate our religion into our lives.

The second factor is concerned more with interaction among the various world religions. Today, because of increasing technological change and the nature of the world economy, we are much more dependent on one another than ever before. Different countries, different continents, have become more closely related to one another. In reality the survival of one region of the world depends on that of others. Therefore, the world has become much closer, much more interdependent. As a result, there is more human interaction on a larger scale. Under such circumstances, the acceptance of pluralism among the world's religions is very important. In previous times, when communities lived separately from one another and religions arose in relative isolation, the idea that there was only one possible religion was very useful. But now the situation has changed, and the circumstances are entirely different. Now, therefore, it is crucial to accept the fact that different religions exist, and in order to develop genuine mutual respect among them, close contact among the various religions is essential. This is the second factor that will enable the world's religions to be effective in benefiting humanity.

When I was in Tibet, I had no contact with people of religious faiths other than Buddhism, so my attitude toward other religions was not very positive. But once I had had the opportunity to meet with people of different faiths and to learn from personal contact and experience, my attitude toward other religions changed. I realized how useful to humanity other religions are, and what potential each has to contribute to a better world. In the last several centuries the various religions have made marvelous contributions toward the betterment of human beings, and even today there are large numbers of followers benefiting from Christianity, Islam, Judaism, Buddhism, Hinduism, and so forth.

To give an example of the value of meeting people of different faiths: My meetings with the late Thomas Merton showed me what a beautiful, wonderful person he was and gave me firsthand insight into the spiritual potential of the Christian faith. On another occasion I met with a Catholic monk in Montserrat, one of Spain's famous monasteries. I was told that this monk had lived for several years as a hermit on a hill just behind the monastery. When I visited the monastery, he came down from his hermitage especially to meet me. As it happened, his English was even worse than mine, and this gave me more courage to speak with him! We remained face to face, and I inquired, "In those years, what were you doing on that hill?"

He looked at me and answered, "Meditation on compassion, on love." As he said those few words, I understood the message through his eyes. I truly developed genuine admiration for this person and for others like him. Such experiences have helped confirm in my mind that all the world's religions have the potential to produce good people, despite their differences of philosophy and doctrine. Each religious tradition has its own wonderful message to convey.

The point here is that for the people who follow those teachings in which the basic faith is in a creator—in God—that approach is very effective for them. Christians, for instance, do not believe in rebirth, and thus do not accept belief in past or future lives. They accept only this life. However, they hold that this very life is created by God, and this idea gives rise in them to a feeling of intimacy with God and dependence on God. What follows from this is the teaching that we should love our fellow human beings. The reasoning is that if we love God, we must love our fellow human beings because they, like us, were created by God. Their future, like ours, depends on the creator; therefore, their situation is like our own. Consequently, the faith of people who tell others to love God but who themselves do not show genuine love toward their fellow human beings is questionable. The person who believes in God and in love for God must demonstrate the sincerity of his or her love of God through love directed toward fellow human beings. This approach is very powerful, isn't it?

Thus, if we examine each religion from various angles in the same way—not simply from our own philosophical position but from several points of view—there can be no doubt that all major religions have the potential to improve human beings. This is obvious. Through close contact with those of other faiths it is possible to develop a broad-minded attitude and mutual respect with regard to other religions. Close contact with different religions helps me to learn new ideas, new practices, and new methods or techniques that I can incorporate into my own practice. Similarly, some of my Christian brothers and sisters have adopted certain Buddhist methods—for example, the practice of one-pointedness of mind as well as techniques to help improve tolerance, compassion, and love. There is great benefit when practitioners of different religions come together for this kind of interchange. In addition to the development of harmony among them, there are other benefits to be gained as well.

Politicians and national leaders frequently talk about coexistence and coming together. Why not we religious people too? I think the time has come. At Assisi, Italy, in 1987, for example, leaders and representatives of various world religions met to pray together, although I am not certain whether *prayer* is the exact word to describe the practice of all these religions accurately. In any case, what is important is that representatives of the various religions come together in one place and, according to their own belief, pray. This is already happening and is, I think, a very positive development. Nevertheless, we still need to apply more effort toward developing harmony and closeness among the world's religions, since without such effort, we will continue to experience the many problems that divide humanity.

If religion were the only remedy for reducing human conflict, but that remedy itself became another source of conflict, it would be disastrous. Today, as in the past, conflicts take place in the name of religion, because of religious differences, and I think this is very, very sad. If we think broadly and deeply however, we will realize that the situation in the past was entirely different from the situation today. We are no longer isolated but are instead interdependent. Today, therefore, it is very important to realize that a close relationship among religions is essential, so that different religious groups may work closely together and make a common effort for the benefit of humankind.

Thus, sincerity and faith in religious practice on the one hand, and religious tolerance and cooperation on the other, comprise this first level of the value of spiritual practice to humanity.

∽ THE SECOND LEVEL OF SPIRITUALITY: COMPASSION AS THE UNIVERSAL RELIGION

The second level of spirituality is that which transcends religious differences, the level of human compassion and affection. The second level is more important than the first because, no matter how wonderful any religion may be, it is still accepted only by a very limited number of people. The majority of the five or six billion human beings on our planet probably do not practice any religion at all. According to their family background they might identify themselves as belonging to one religious group or another—"I am Hindu," "I am Buddhist," "I am Christian"—but deep down, most of these individuals are not necessarily practitioners of any religious faith. That is all right; whether or not a person embraces a religion is that person's right as an individual. All the great ancient masters, such as Buddha, Mahavira, Jesus, and Mohammed, failed to make the entire human population spiritual-minded. The fact is that nobody can do that. Whether those nonbelievers are called atheists does not matter. Indeed, according to some Western scholars, Buddhists are also atheists, since they do not accept a creator. Therefore, I sometimes add one more word to describe these nonbelievers, and that is *extreme*; I call them extreme nonbelievers. They are not only nonbelievers but are extreme in their view that spirituality in any form has no value. However, we must remember that these people are also a part of humanity, and that they also, like all human beings, have the desire to be happy—to have a happy and peaceful life. This is the important point.

I believe that it is all right to remain a nonbeliever, but as long as you are a part of humanity, as long as you are a human being, you need human affection, human compassion. This is the essential teaching of all the religious traditions. Without human compassion, even religious beliefs can become destructive. Thus, the essential practice, whether you are religious or not, is a good heart. I consider human affection and compassion the universal religion. Whether a believer or a nonbeliever, everyone needs human affection and compassion, because compassion gives us inner strength, hope, and mental peace. Thus, compassion is indispensable for everyone.

As I mentioned, some of my Christian brothers and sisters, both monks and lay people, have told me that they are using Buddhist techniques and methods to develop their compassion and even their Christian faith. I always tell my Western friends it is best to try and keep your own tradition. Changing your religion is not easy and sometimes causes confusion.

However, those individuals who really feel the Buddhist approach is more effective and more suitable to their mental disposition should think about it very carefully. Once you are fully convinced that

Buddhism is right for you, then you are free to follow it. The important thing to remember is this: sometimes people develop a critical
attitude toward their previous religion or tradition in order to justify
having changed their faith. This you must avoid. Your previous religion may no longer be effective for you, but that does not mean it is
of no use to humanity. In recognition of other people's views and
rights, and the value of their traditions, you must honor your previous religion. This is very important.

5

Basic Buddhism

WHILE I BELIEVE that human compassion and affection are universal values that transcend the boundaries of religious difference, the significance of compassion within Buddhism is grounded in a particular worldview, with goals and methods. This worldview lays out not only what I have explained previously about the benefits of compassion and the methods for developing it, but it also shows how the development of compassion is integral to the Buddhist understanding of reality and the path to enlightenment. It may be helpful then for me to provide some explanation of Buddhist philosophy.

THE FOUR NOBLE TRUTHS AND CAUSATION

The core teachings of the Buddha are grounded in the four noble truths. These are the foundation of the Buddhist teaching. The four noble truths are the truth of suffering, its origin, the possibility of cessation of suffering, and the path leading to that cessation. The teachings on the four noble truths are based in human experience, underlying which is the natural aspiration to seek happiness and to avoid suffering. The happiness that we desire and the suffering that we shun are not random but rather come about through causes and conditions. Understanding this causal mechanism of suffering and happiness is what the four noble truths are about.

In order to understand the causal mechanism behind our suffering and happiness, we have to carefully analyze causation. For example, you might think that your experiences of pain and suffering and happiness happen for no reason—in other words, that they have no cause. Buddhist teachings say this is not possible. Perhaps you think that your suffering and happiness are, in some sense, caused by a transcendent being. This possibility is also rejected in Buddhism. Maybe you think that a primal substance could be the original source of all things. Buddhist teachings reject this possibility, too. Using reasons to eliminate these possibilities, Buddhism concludes that our experiences of suffering and happiness do not come about by themselves or because of some independently existing cause, nor are they the product of some combination of these. Instead, Buddhist teaching understands causation in terms of what is called *interdependent origination:* all things and events, including our experiences of suffering and happiness, arise from the coming together of a multiplicity of causes and conditions.

❧ UNDERSTANDING THE PRIMARY ROLE OF MIND

If we probe the teaching of the four noble truths carefully, we discover the primary importance that consciousness, or mind, plays in determining our experiences of suffering and happiness. The Buddhist view is that there are different levels of suffering. For example, there is the suffering that is very obvious to all of us, such as painful experiences. This we all can recognize as suffering. A second level of suffering includes what we ordinarily define as pleasurable sensations. In reality, pleasurable sensations are suffering because they have the seed of dissatisfaction within them. There is also a third level of suffering, which in Buddhist terminology is called the pervasive suffering of conditioning. One might say that this third level of suffering is the mere fact of our existence as unenlightened beings who are subject to negative emotions, thoughts, and karmic actions. *Karma* means action and is what keeps us stuck in a negative cycle. Being bound to karma in this way is the third type of suffering.

If you look at these three different kinds of suffering, you will find that all of them are ultimately grounded in states of mind. In fact, undisciplined states of mind in and of themselves are suffering. If we look at the origin of suffering in the Buddhist texts, we find that, although we read about karma and the delusion that motivates karmic action, we are dealing with actions committed by an agent. Because there is always a motive behind every action, karma can also be understood ultimately in terms of a state of mind, an undisciplined state of mind. Similarly, when we talk about delusions that propel one into acting in negative ways, these are also undisciplined states of mind. Therefore, when Buddhists refer to the truth of the origin of suffering, we are talking about a state of mind that is undisciplined and untamed, one that obscures us from enlightenment and causes us to suffer. The origin of suffering, the cause of suffering, and the suffering itself can all be understood ultimately only in terms of a state of mind.

When we talk about the cessation of suffering, we are speaking only in relation to a living being, an agent with consciousness. Buddhist teachings describe cessation of suffering as the highest state of happiness. This happiness should not be understood in terms of pleasurable sensations; we are not talking about happiness at the level of feeling or sensation. Rather, we are referring to the highest level of happiness: total freedom from suffering and delusion. Again, this is a state of mind, a level of realization.

Ultimately, in order to understand our experience of suffering and pain and the path that leads to cessation—the four noble truths—we have to understand the nature of mind.

❧ MIND AND NIRVANA

The process by which mind creates the suffering we live in is described by the Indian master Chandrakirti in his *Guide to the Middle Way* when he states, "An undisciplined state of mind gives rise to delusions that propel an individual into negative action, which then creates the negative environment in which the person lives."

To try to understand the nature of freedom from suffering, what Buddhists call *nirvana,* we can look at a passage in Nagarjuna's famous *Fundamentals of the Middle Way* where he equates, in some sense, unenlightened existence *(samsara)* and enlightened existence (nirvana). The point Nagarjuna makes is that we should not think there is an intrinsic, essential nature to our existence, be it enlightened or unenlightened. From the point of view of emptiness, they are equally devoid of any kind of intrinsic reality. That which differentiates an unenlightened state from an enlightened state is the knowledge and the experience of emptiness. The knowledge and experience of the emptiness of samsara is itself nirvana. The difference between samsara and nirvana is a state of mind.

So, given these premises, it is fair to ask: Is Buddhism suggesting that everything is nothing but a projection of our mind? This is a critical question and one that has elicited different responses from Buddhist teachers throughout the history of Buddhism. In one camp, great masters have argued that in the final analysis everything, including our experience of suffering and happiness, is nothing but a projection of our mind.

But there is another camp that has vehemently argued against this extreme form of subjectivism. This second camp maintains that although one can, in some sense, understand everything, including one's experiences, as creations of one's mind, this does not mean that everything is only the mind. They argue that one must maintain a degree of objectivity and believe that things do in fact exist. Although this camp also maintains that consciousness plays a role in creating our experience and the world, there is at the same time an objective world.

There is another point that I think one should understand with regard to the Buddhist concept of nirvana. Nagabuddhi, a student of Nagarjuna, states that: "Enlightenment or spiritual freedom is not a gift that someone can give to you, nor is the seed for enlightenment something that is owned by someone else." The implication here is that the potential for enlightenment exists naturally in all of us. Nagarjuna's student goes on to ask, "What is nirvana, what is enlightenment, what is spiritual freedom?" He then answers, "True enlighten-ment is nothing but when the nature of one's own self is fully real-ized." This nature of one's own self is what Buddhists call the ultimate clear light, or inner radiant nature of the mind. When this is fully actualized, or realized, that is enlightenment, that is true buddhahood.

We can see that when we talk about enlightenment and nirvana, which are fruits of one's spiritual endeavors, we are speaking about a state of mind. Similarly, when we talk about the delusions that obstruct our actualization of that enlightened state, we are also talk-ing about states of mind—deluded states of mind. In particular, we are referring to the delusions that are grounded in a distorted way of per-ceiving one's own self and the world. The only way we can eliminate that misunderstanding, that distorted way of perceiving the self and the world, is through cultivating insight into the true nature of mind.

In summary, the teachings of the Buddha equate, on the one hand, an undisciplined state of mind with suffering and, on the other hand, a disciplined state of mind with happiness and spiritual free-dom. This is an essential point.

❧ VALID AND INVALID THOUGHT

Mind in Buddhism has a broad meaning that encompasses the whole spectrum of conscious experience, including all thoughts and emotions.

One natural fact—I suppose one could call it a psychological law—of our subjective experience is that two directly opposing thoughts or emotions cannot coexist at the same time. From our ordinary day-to-day experience, we know that there are thoughts that can be classified as valid and others that are invalid. For example, if a particular thought corresponds to reality, that is, if there is a correspondence between a state of affairs in the world and one's perception of it, then one can call that a valid thought or a valid experience. But we also experience thoughts and emotions that are completely contrary to the way things are. In some cases, they may be forms of exaggeration, but in other cases they may be diametrically opposed to the way things really are. These thoughts and emotions can be called invalid.

Buddhist texts, especially those dealing with ways of knowing, draw on this distinction between valid and invalid thoughts and emotions to discuss valid cognition and its results. The point here is that for an endeavor to be successful and lead to the achievement of an objective, valid thoughts and emotions are required.

In Buddhist texts, the attainment of the highest spiritual liberation is said to be the fruit of valid thoughts and emotions. For example, according to Buddhist teachings, the principal factor that gives rise to enlightenment is said to be true insight into the nature of reality. True insight into the nature of reality is a valid way of knowing things, such as the nature of the world. Compassion, altruism, and *bodhichitta*—the mind of enlightenment—are integral parts of this true insight into reality, and thus, these are all based on valid thought. Although altruism and compassion are more emotions than cognitive thoughts, the process that leads to the realization of universal compassion and bodhichitta involves comparing truths and falsehoods. This is a process of cultivating valid ways of seeing and experiencing things. Therefore, we can say that buddhahood itself is a consequence of valid thoughts and emotions. In contrast, we can see unenlightened experience (samsara) as the product of invalid ways of experiencing.

For example, according to Buddhism, the fundamental root of our unenlightened existence and suffering is ignorance. The primary characteristic of this ignorance is a distorted perception of the world and of ourselves. Once again, invalid thoughts and emotions, invalid ways of seeing and experiencing things and ourselves, are ultimately the source of our suffering and unenlightenment. In the final analysis, valid thoughts and emotions correlate to happiness and spiritual freedom, while invalid thoughts and emotions correlate to suffering and the unenlightened state.

❧ THE TWO TRUTHS

In training the mind, we develop, enhance, and perfect valid thoughts and emotions, and we counteract, undermine, and eventually eliminate invalid forms. The multiple approaches to training the mind have two principal aspects. One is the development of insight or wisdom, that is, developing these valid ways of thinking. The other aspect is method, or *skillful means*. This way of looking at the essence of the teachings of the Buddha as teachings on wisdom and on method corresponds wonderfully to a point Nagarjuna makes. He says that all the teachings of the Buddha must be understood via the two truths, conventional truth and ultimate truth. One has to understand the essential teachings of the four noble truths in terms of these two truths. When we talk about the nature of the two truths, however, we should understand that they are not two independent and unrelated realms.

The various philosophical schools have different understandings of these two truths. When I talk about the two truths, my understanding is grounded on the perspective of the Indian Madhyamika thinkers, toward whom I have a particular bias based on admiration. According to the Madhyamika view, conventional reality is constituted by ordinary experience in the realm of cause and effect. This is the realm of multiplicity where we see the diverse laws of reality at work. This level of reality is called conventional truth because the truth of our experiences at this level is specific to a conventional, or normal, way of understanding the world.

If we probe deeper, we find that each and every thing is the result of many causes and conditions. The origination of things and events is dependent upon multiple factors. What is the implication of this reality of interdependence? It is that no thing or event, including one's own self, possesses an independent or intrinsic reality. This absence of an independent reality is said to be ultimate truth. The reason it is called *ultimate* truth is that it is not obvious to us at our ordinary level of perception of the world. One needs to probe deeper to find it.

These two truths are really two sides of the same thing—two perspectives on one and the same world. The principle of two truths is very important because it directly touches upon our understanding of the relationship between our perception and the reality of the world. We find in the Indian Buddhist literature a tremendous amount of discussion, debate, and analysis concerning how the mind, or consciousness, perceives the world. Questions arise such as: What is the nature of the relationship between our subjective experience and the objective world? and: To what extent are our experiences constituted by the world we perceive? I think the reason there has been such tremendous discussion in Buddhism about these questions is because the answers to them play such a crucial role in the development of one's mind.

⤫ THE TWO ASPECTS OF BUDDHAHOOD

Corresponding to these two levels of reality are the two dimensions of the path, method and wisdom. And because there are two principal dimensions to the path there are two aspects to the resultant state of buddhahood. One is the form body of a buddha, and the other is the truth body, the actual reality of an enlightened mind.

The form body is said to be that aspect of a fully enlightened being that exists purely in relation to others. By assuming such diverse forms and appearances, a fully enlightened being can engage in all kinds of activities to ensure the well-being of others. The truth body of a buddha is said to be the aspect that exists in relation to other buddhas. The reason for this is that the truth body is directly accessible only to a fully enlightened being. It is only by assuming a form body that the truth body can manifest and engage in activities that are beneficial to unenlightened beings. So the state of buddhahood can therefore be seen as the fulfillment of both one's own self-interest and the interests of others.

To become a buddha means that one has both fully ascertained the true nature of reality and developed fully the wish to benefit others. A buddha is therefore a complete manifestation of both wisdom and compassion.

6

The Bodhisattva Way

THE *Guide to the Bodhisattva's Way of Life* by the eighth-century Indian master Shantideva is the primary source of most of the literature on the altruistic attitude of putting the happiness of others before our own. I received an oral transmission of this text from the late Khunu Rinpoche, a remarkable teacher from Kinnaur in northern India. I myself try to apply these teachings as much as possible and also, whenever the opportunity arises, explain them to others. Using Shantideva's text as a guide, I would like to explore some of the main points of this compassionate practice.

RECOGNIZING THE ENEMY WITHIN

In order to prioritize the well-being of others, it is first necessary to recognize what keeps us stuck in the self-centered attitude.

Shantideva explains in the fourth chapter, entitled "Conscientious-ness," that the delusions within our minds, such as hatred, anger, attachment, and jealousy, are our true enemies. As he states in the two verses below, these enemies do not have physical bodies with legs and arms, nor do they hold weapons in their hands; instead, they reside in our minds and afflict us from within. They control us from within and bind us to them as their slaves. Normally, however, we do not realize these delusions as our enemies, and so we never confront or challenge them. Since we do not challenge them, they reside un-threatened within our mind and continue to inflict harm on us at will.

> The enemies such as hatred and craving
> Have neither arms nor legs,
> And are neither courageous nor wise;
> How, then, have I been used like a slave by them?
>
> For while they dwell within my mind,
> At their pleasure they cause me harm;
> Yet I patiently endure them without anger.
> But this is an inappropriate and shameful time
> for patience. (4:28–29)

Negative thoughts and emotions are often deceptive. They play tricks on us. Desire, for example, appears to us as a trusted friend, something beautiful and dear to us. Similarly, anger and hatred appear to us like our protectors or reliable bodyguards. Sometimes, when someone is about to harm you, anger rises up like a protector and gives you a kind of strength. Even though you may be physically weaker than your assailant, anger makes you feel strong. It gives you a false sense of power and energy, the result being, in this case, that you might get yourself beaten up. Because anger and other destructive emotions appear in such deceptive guises, we rarely actually challenge them. There are many similar ways in which the negative thoughts and emotions deceive us. In order to fully realize the treachery of these negative thoughts and emotions, we must first achieve some mental stability. Only then will we begin to see their treacherous nature.

Despite being a monk and a supposed practitioner of the *Guide to the Bodhisattva's Way of Life,* I myself still occasionally become irritated and angry and, as a result, use harsh words toward others. Then, a few moments later when the anger has subsided, I feel embarrassed; the negative words are already spoken, and there is truly no way to take them back. Although the words themselves are uttered and the sound of the voice has ceased to exist, their impact lives on. Hence, the only thing I can do is to go to the person and apologize. But in the meantime, I may feel quite shy and embarrassed. This shows that even a short instance of anger and irritation creates a great amount of discomfort and disturbance to the one who gets angry, not to mention the harm caused to the person who is the target of that anger. So in reality, these negative states of mind obscure our intelligence and good judgment and thereby cause great damage.

One of the best human qualities is our intelligence, which enables us to judge what is wholesome and what is unwholesome, what is beneficial and what is harmful. Negative thoughts, such as anger and strong attachment, destroy this special human quality; this is indeed very sad. When anger or attachment dominates the mind, a person becomes almost crazed, and I am certain that nobody wishes to be crazy. Under the power of anger or attachment we commit all kinds of harmful acts—often having far-reaching and destructive consequences. A person gripped by such states of mind and emotion is like a blind person, who cannot see where he is going. Yet we neglect to challenge these negative thoughts and emotions that lead us nearly to insanity. On the contrary, we often nurture and reinforce them! By doing this we are, in fact, making ourselves prey to their destructive power. When you reflect along these lines, you will realize that our true enemy is not outside ourselves.

Let me give you another example. When your mind is trained in self-discipline, even if you are surrounded by hostile forces, your peace of mind will hardly be disturbed. On the other hand, if your mind is undisciplined, your mental peace and calm can easily be disrupted by your own negative thoughts and emotions. So I repeat, the real enemy is within, not outside. Usually we define our enemy as a person, an external agent, whom we believe is causing harm to us or to someone we hold dear. But such an enemy is dependent on many conditions and is impermanent. One moment, the person may act as an enemy; at yet another moment, he or she may become your best friend. This is a truth that we often experience in our own lives. But negative thoughts and emotions, the inner enemy, will always remain the enemy. They are your enemy today, they have been your enemy in the past, and they will remain your enemy in the future as long as they reside within your mind.

This inner enemy is extremely dangerous. The destructive potential of an external enemy is limited when compared to that of its inner counterpart. Moreover, it is often possible to create a physical defense against an external enemy. In the past, for example, even though they had limited material resources and technological capabilities, people defended themselves by building fortresses and castles with many layers of walls. With today's powerfully destructive weapons, such defenses are of course obsolete. In a time when every country is a potential target for the nuclear weapons of others, human beings still continue to develop defense systems of greater and greater sophistication. The missile defense system proposed by the United States is a typical example of such an initiative. Underlying its development is still the old belief that we can eventually create a system that will provide us with the "ultimate" protection. I do not know if it will ever be possible to create a defense system capable of guaranteeing world-wide protection against all external forces of destruction. However, one thing is certain: as long as those destructive internal enemies of anger and hatred are left to themselves unchallenged, the threat of physical annihilation will always loom over us. In fact, the destructive power of an external enemy ultimately derives from the power of these internal forces. The inner enemy is the trigger that unleashes the destructive power of the external enemy. Shantideva tells us that as long as these inner enemies remain secure within, there is great danger.

Shantideva goes on to say that even if everyone in the world were to stand up against you as your enemies and harm you, as long as your own mind was disciplined and calm, they would not be able to disturb your peace. Yet a single instance of delusion arising in your mind has the power to disturb that peace and inner stability.

Should even all the gods and demigods
Rise up against me as my enemies,
They could neither lead nor place me
In the roaring fires of deepest hell.

But the mighty foe, these disturbing conceptions,
In a moment, can cast me amidst those flames,
Which when met will cause not even the ashes
Of the king of mountains to remain. (4:30–31)

Shantideva also states that one crucial difference between the ordinary enemy and the delusions is that if you relate in a friendly manner and with understanding toward the ordinary enemy, then you might be able to change that enemy into a friend, but you cannot relate to the delusions in a similar way. The more you try to associate with them with the aim of befriending them, the more harmful and disastrous they become.

If I agreeably honor and entrust myself to others,
They will bring me benefit and happiness;
But if I entrust myself to these disturbing conceptions,
In the future they will bring only misery and harm. (4:33)

As long as you remain under the domination of the delusions and their underlying states of ignorance, you have no possibility of achieving genuine, lasting happiness. This, I think, is a natural fact. If you feel deeply disturbed by this truth, you should respond by seeking a state of freedom from it—that is, the state of nirvana. Those who become monks and nuns take the attainment of nirvana, or true liberation, as the focus of their lives. So if you can afford to devote yourself wholly to the practice of Dharma, then you should implement the spiritual methods in your life that lead to the attainment of this state of freedom. If, as in my own case, you do not have sufficient time, it is quite difficult, isn't it? I know that one factor preventing me from devoting myself fully to such a committed way of life is my own laziness. I am a rather lazy Dalai Lama, the lazy Tenzin Gyatso! Even if you cannot lead a single-minded life of Dharma practice, it is very beneficial to reflect on these teachings as much as possible and make efforts to recognize the transience of all adverse circumstances. Like ripples in a pool, they occur and soon disappear.

Insofar as our lives are conditioned by our past deluded actions, they are characterized by endless cycles of problems, which arise and then subside. One problem appears and passes, and soon another one begins. They come and go in a ceaseless continuum. However, the continuum of each of our consciousnesses—for example, Tenzin Gyatso's consciousness—is beginningless. Though in a state of constant flux, an ever-changing, dynamic process, the basic nature of consciousness never changes. Such is the nature of our conditioned existence, and the realization of this truth makes it easy for me to relate to reality. This realistic outlook helps me maintain my peace and calm. This is the monk Tenzin Gyatso's way of thinking. Through my own experience, I know that the mind can be trained, and by means of that training, we can bring about a profound change within ourselves. That much, I know, is quite certain.

Despite its pervasive influence and destructive potential, there is one particular way in which the inner enemy is weaker than the external enemy. Shantideva explains in the *Guide to the Bodhisattva's Way of Life* that to overcome ordinary enemies you need physical strength and weapons. You might even need to spend billions of dollars on weapons to counter them. But to combat the enemy within, the disturbing conceptions, you need only develop the factors that give rise to the wisdom realizing the ultimate nature of phenomena. You do not need any material weapon nor do you need physical strength. This is very true.

> Deluded disturbing conceptions! If forsaken by the
>   wisdom eye
> And dispelled from my mind, where could you go?
> Where could you dwell in order to be able to injure
>   me again?
> But, weak-minded, I have been reduced to making
>   no effort. (4:46)

Actually, when I was receiving the oral teachings on this text from the late Khunu Rinpoche, I remarked that the *Guide to the Bodhisattva's Way of Life* states that delusions are humble and weak, which is not true. He immediately responded by saying that you do not need an atom bomb to destroy the delusions! So this is what Shantideva means here. You do not need expensive sophisticated weapons to destroy the inner enemy. You simply need to develop a firm determination to defeat them by generating wisdom: a realization of the true nature of the mind. You must also genuinely understand both the relative nature of negative thoughts and emotions as well as the ultimate nature of all phenomena. In technical Buddhist terminology, this insight is known as the *true insight into the nature of emptiness.* Shantideva mentions still another sense in which the inner enemy is weaker. Unlike an external enemy, the inner enemy cannot regroup and launch a comeback once it has been destroyed from within.

❧ OVERCOMING ANGER AND HATRED

We have discussed the deceptive and destructive nature of the delusions. Hatred and anger are the greatest obstacles for a practitioner of bodhichitta, the altruistic wish for enlightenment. Bodhisattvas should never generate hatred, but instead, they should counteract it. For this purpose, the practice of patience, or tolerance, is crucial.

Shantideva begins the sixth chapter of his text, entitled "Patience," by explaining the seriousness of the harm and damage caused by anger and hatred: they harm us now and in the future, and they also harm us by destroying our collection of past merits. Since the practitioner of patience must counteract and overcome hatred, Shantideva emphasizes the importance of first identifying the factors that cause anger and hatred. The principal causes are dissatisfaction and unhappiness. When we are unhappy and dissatisfied, we easily become frustrated and this leads to feelings of hatred and anger.

Shantideva explains that it is very important for those of us training in patience to prevent mental unhappiness from arising—as is prone to occur when you feel that you or your loved ones are threatened, or when misfortune befalls you, or when others obstruct your goals. Your feelings of dissatisfaction and unhappiness on these occasions are the fuel that feeds hatred and anger. So right from the beginning, it is important not to allow such circumstances to disturb your peace of mind.

He emphasizes that we should, with all the means at our disposal, counteract and eliminate the onset of hatred, since its only function is to harm us and others. This is very profound advice.

> Having found its fuel of dissatisfaction
> In the prevention of what I wish for

And in the doing of what I do not want,

Hatred increases and then destroys me. (6:7)

If maintaining a balanced and happy state of mind even in the face of adversity is a key factor in preventing hatred from arising, we still may wonder how to achieve it. Shantideva says that when you are faced with adverse circumstances, feeling unhappy serves no purpose in overcoming the undesirable situation. It is not only futile but will, in fact, only serve to aggravate your own anxiety and bring about an uncomfortable and dissatisfied state of mind. You lose all sense of composure and happiness. Anxiety and unhappiness gradually eat away inside you and affect your sleep patterns, your appetite, and your health as well. In fact, if the initial harm you experienced was inflicted by an enemy, your mental unhappiness may even become a source of delight for that person. Therefore, it is pointless to feel unhappy and dissatisfied when faced with adverse circumstances or, for that matter, to retaliate against whomever caused you harm.

Generally, there are two types of hatred or anger that result from unhappiness and dissatisfaction. One type is when someone inflicts harm upon you, and as a result you feel unhappy and generate anger. Another type is when, although no person may be directly inflicting harm upon you, as a result of seeing the success and prosperity of your enemies, you feel unhappy and generate anger on that basis.

Similarly, there are generally two types of harm caused by others. One type is direct physical harm inflicted by others and consciously experienced by you. The other type is harm done to your material possessions, reputation, friendship, and so on. Though not directed at your body, these acts are also a type of harm. Let us say that a person hits you with a stick, and you feel pain and become angry. You don't feel angry toward the stick, do you? What exactly is the object of your anger? If it would be appropriate to feel angry toward the factor that impelled the act of hitting, then you should not be angry with the person but with the negative emotions that compelled that person to act. Ordinarily, however, we do not make such distinctions. Instead, we consider the person—the intermediary agent between the negative emotions and the act—as solely responsible, and we hold a grudge against him or her, not against the stick or the delusions.

We should also be aware that since we possess a physical body that is susceptible to pain when hit by a stick, our own body partly contributes to our experience of pain. Because of our body and its nature, we sometimes experience physical pain even when no external causes of pain are present. It is clear then that the experience of pain or suffering comes about as a result of interaction between both our own body and various external factors.

You can also reflect on how, if it is the essential nature of the person who is harming you to inflict harm on others, there is no point in being angry, since there would be nothing that you or that person could do to change their essential nature. If it were truly the person's nature to inflict harm, the person would simply be unable to act otherwise. As stated by Shantideva:

> Even if it were the nature of the childish
> To cause harm to other beings,
> It would still be incorrect to be angry with them.
> For this would be like begrudging fire for having
>   the nature to burn. (6:39)

On the other hand, if harming is not the person's essential nature, but instead their apparently harmful character is merely incidental and circumstantial, then there is still no need to feel angry toward that person since the problem is entirely due to certain immediate conditions and circumstances. For example, he may have lost his temper and acted badly, even though he did not really mean to hurt you. It is possible to think along these lines as well.

When you feel angry toward others who are not causing you direct, physical harm but whom you perceive as getting in the way of your acquisition of fame, position, material gains, and so forth, you should think in the following manner: Why should I get especially upset or angry about this particular problem? Analyze the nature of what you are being kept from obtaining—fame and so on—and examine carefully their benefit to you. Are they really that important? You will find that they are not. Since that is the case, why be so angry toward that person? Thinking in this way is also useful.

When you become angry as a result of the unhappiness you feel at seeing your enemies' success and prosperity, you should remember that simply being hateful, angry, or unhappy is not going to affect that person's material possessions or success in life. Therefore, even from that point of view, it is quite pointless.

In addition to the practice of patience, those practitioners who take Shantideva's text as inspiration are also seeking to develop bodhichitta—the wish to achieve enlightenment for the benefit of all sentient beings—as well as compassion and mind training. If, despite their practice, they still feel unhappy about their enemies' success in life, then they should remember that this attitude is very inappropriate for a practitioner of compassion. If this negative attitude persists, the thought "I am a practitioner of compassion; I am someone who lives according to the precepts of mind training" becomes mere words devoid of meaning. Instead, a true practitioner of bodhichitta should rejoice that others have been able to achieve something on their own without one's help. Rather than being unhappy and hateful, we should rejoice in the success of others.

If we investigate on a still deeper level, we will find that when enemies inflict harm on us, we can actually feel gratitude toward them. Such situations provide us with rare opportunities to put to test our own practice of patience. It is a precious occasion to practice not only patience but the other bodhisattva ideals as well. As a result, we have the opportunity to accumulate merit in these situations and to receive the benefits thereof. The poor enemy, on the other hand, because of the negative action of inflicting harm on someone out of anger and hatred, must eventually face the negative consequences of his or her own actions. It is almost as if the perpetrators of the harm sacrifice themselves for the sake of our benefit. Since the merit accumulated from the practice of patience was possible only because of the opportunity provided us by our enemy, strictly speaking, we should dedicate our merit to the benefit of that enemy. This is why the *Guide to the Bodhisattva's Way of Life* speaks of the kindness of the enemy.

Although we might recognize, on the one hand, the kindness of the enemy, we might feel, on the other, that the enemy had no intention to be kind to us. Therefore, we think, it is not necessary for us to remember his or her kindness at all. If, in order to respect or hold something dear, there must be conscious intent from the side of the object, then this argument should apply equally to other subjects as well. For example, from their sides, the true cessation of suffering and the true path leading to cessation—the third and fourth noble truths—have no conscious intention to be beneficial. Yet as Buddhists we still respect and revere them. Why? Because we derive benefit from them. If the benefits we derive justify our reverence and respect for these two truths, despite their not having any conscious intention, then this same rationale should apply to the enemy as well.

However, you might feel that there is a major difference between the enemy and these two truths of true cessation and true path. Unlike the two truths, the enemy has a conscious will to harm you. But this difference is also not a valid reason not to respect the enemy. In fact, if anything, it is additional grounds to revere and be grateful to your enemy. It is indeed this special factor that makes your enemy unique. If the mere inflicting of physical pain were sufficient to make someone an enemy, you would have to consider your doctor an enemy, for he often causes pain during treatment. Now, as a genuine practitioner of compassion and bodhichitta, you must develop patience. And in order to practice sincerely and to develop patience, you need someone who willfully hurts you. Thus, these people give us real opportunities to practice these things. They are testing our inner strength in a way that even our guru cannot. Even the Buddha possesses no such potential. Therefore, the enemy is *the only one* who gives us this golden opportunity. That is a remarkable conclusion, isn't it! By thinking along these lines and using these reasons, you will eventually develop a kind of extraordinary respect toward your enemies. This is Shantideva's primary message in the sixth chapter.

Once you generate genuine respect toward your enemy, you can then easily remove most of the major obstacles to developing infinite altruism. Shantideva mentions that, just as the many buddhas help us achieve enlightenment, there is an equal contribution from ordinary sentient beings as well. Enlightenment can only be achieved in reliance upon both of these: the kindness of sentient beings, and the kindness of the buddhas.

For those of us who claim to be followers of Buddha Shakyamuni and who revere and respect the bodhisattva ideals, Shantideva states that it is incorrect to hold grudges or have hatred toward our enemies, when all the buddhas and bodhisattvas hold all sentient beings dear to their hearts. Of course, our enemies are included within the field of all sentient beings. If we hold grudges toward those whom the buddhas and bodhisattvas hold close to their hearts, we contradict the ideals and experience of the buddhas and bodhisattvas, those very beings whom we are trying to emulate.

Even in worldly terms, the more respect and affection we feel toward people, the more consideration we have for them. We try to avoid acting in ways that they might disapprove of, thinking that we might offend them. We try to take into consideration our friends' ways of thinking, their principles, and so on. If we do this even for our ordinary friends, then, as practitioners of the bodhisattva ideals, we should show the same, if not higher, regard for the buddhas and bodhisattvas by trying to not hold grudges and hateful feelings toward our enemies.

Shantideva concludes this chapter on patience by explaining the benefits of practicing patience. In summary, through practicing patience, not only will you reach a state of omniscience in the future, but even in your everyday life you will experience its practical benefits. You will be able to maintain your peace of mind and live a joyful life.

When we practice patience to overcome hatred and anger, it is important to be equipped with the force of joyous effort. We should be skillful in cultivating joyous effort. Shantideva explains that, just as we must be mindful when undertaking a mundane task, such as waging war, to inflict the greatest possible destruction on the enemy while at the same time protecting ourselves from the enemy's harm, in the same way, when we undertake the practice of joyous effort, it is important to attain the greatest level of success while assuring that this action does not damage or hinder our other practices.

❧ ONESELF AND OTHERS: EXCHANGING PLACES

In the chapter on meditation in the *Guide to the Bodhisattva's Way of Life,* we find an explanation of the actual meditation for cultivating compassion and bodhichitta. The explanation follows a method called *equalizing and exchanging oneself and others*. Equalizing and exchanging oneself and others means developing the attitude that understands that, "Just as I desire happiness and wish to avoid suffering, the same is true of all other living beings, who are infinite as space; they too desire happiness and wish to avoid suffering." Just as we work for our own benefit in order to gain happiness and protect ourselves from suffering, we should also work for the benefit of others, to help them attain happiness and freedom from suffering.

Although there are different parts to our body, such as our head, limbs, and so on, insofar as the need to protect them is concerned, there is no difference among them, for they are all equally parts of the same body. In the same manner, all sentient beings have this natural tendency—wishing to attain happiness and be free from suffering—and, insofar as that natural inclination is concerned, there is no difference whatsoever between sentient beings. Consequently, we should not discriminate between ourselves and others as we work to gain happiness and overcome suffering.

We should reflect upon and make serious efforts to dissolve our view that we and others are separate and distinct. We have seen that insofar as the wish to gain happiness and to avoid suffering is concerned, there is no difference at all. The same is also true of our *natural right* to be happy; just as we have the right to enjoy happiness and freedom from suffering, all other living beings have the same natural right. So wherein lies the difference? The difference lies in the number of sentient beings involved. When we speak of the welfare of ourselves, we are speaking of the welfare of only one individual, whereas the welfare of others encompasses the well-being of an infinite number of beings. From that point of view, we can understand that others' welfare is much more important than our own.

If our own and others' welfare were totally unrelated and independent of one another, we could make a case for neglecting others' welfare. But that is not the case. I am always related to others and heavily dependent on them, no matter what my level of spiritual development: while I am unenlightened, while I am on the path, and also once I have achieved enlightenment. If we reflect along these lines, the importance of working for the benefit of others becomes naturally apparent.

You should also examine whether, by remaining selfish and self-centered despite the above points, you can still achieve happiness and fulfill your desires. If you could do so, then pursuit of your selfish and self-centered habits would be a reasonable course of action. But it is not. The nature of our existence is such that we must depend on the cooperation and kindness of others for our survival. It is an observable fact that the more we take the welfare of others to heart and work for their benefit, the more benefit we attain for ourselves.

You can see this fact for yourself. On the other hand, the more self-ish and self-centered you remain, the more lonely and miserable you become. You can also observe this fact yourself.

Therefore, if you definitely want to work for your own benefit and welfare, then it is better to take into account the welfare of others and to regard their welfare as more important than your own. By contemplating these points, you will certainly be able to strengthen more and more your attitude of cherishing the well-being of others.

Furthermore, we can complement our practice of compassion and bodhichitta with meditations on the various factors of wisdom. For example, we can reflect upon buddha-nature: the potential to actualize buddhahood that resides within ourselves and all sentient beings. We can also reflect on the ultimate nature of phenomena, their empty nature, by using logical reasoning to ascertain the nature of reality. We can reflect that the cessation of suffering is possible because the ignorance that is its root cause is by nature adventitious and, hence, can be separated from the essentially pure nature of our mind. By thinking and meditating on the factors of wisdom and maintaining a sustained practice of compassion and altruism with concerted effort over a long period of time, you will see a real change in your mind.

7

Eight Verses for Training the Mind

ALL THE DIVERSE TEACHINGS of the Buddha provide methods for training and transforming the mind. Historically, however, a traditional class of practices and the literature associated with them developed in Tibet known as *lojong,* which means "mind training." These practices are so called because they aim at nothing short of bringing about a radical transformation in our thinking and, through it, helping us to live a compassionate life. One of the principal characteristics of lojong practice is the emphasis it places on overcoming our deluded grasping at a solid ego and the self-cherishing attitudes based on this misapprehension of self. The self-cherishing attitude obstructs our generation of genuine empathy toward others and limits our outlook to the narrow confines of our own self-centered concerns. In essence, with mind training, we seek to transform our normal selfish outlook on life into a more altruistic one, which, at the very least, regards the welfare of others as equal in importance to our own, and ideally regards others' welfare as much more important than ours.

One particularly important piece of mind-training literature is *Eight Verses for Training the Mind* by the twelfth-century master Langri Tangpa. *Eight Verses for Training the Mind* summarizes the key teachings on both wisdom and method. It focuses on the antidotes that enable the practitioner to counter the two principal obstacles. The first obstacle is the self-cherishing attitude, and the antidotes for this are chiefly the cultivation of altruism, compassion, and bodhichitta. The second obstacle is our deluded grasping at some kind of enduring, permanently existing self. The antidote to this is contained in the wisdom teachings. The first seven verses of *Eight Verses for Training the Mind* deal with the practices associated with cultivating method, and the eighth verse deals with the practices for cultivating wisdom. These eight verses can therefore be said to contain the entire essence of the Buddha's teachings in a distinct form.

1   By thinking of all sentient beings
      as even better than the wish-granting gem
      for accomplishing the highest aim,
      may I always consider them precious.

These four lines are about cultivating a sense of holding dear all other sentient beings. The main point this verse emphasizes is to develop an attitude that enables you to regard other sentient beings as precious, much as we might regard precious jewels.

In this verse, there is an explicit reference to the agent "I": "May *I* always consider others precious." Perhaps a brief discussion on the Buddhist understanding of what this "I" is referring to might be helpful.

Generally speaking, no one disputes that people—you, me, others—exist. We do not question the existence of someone who undergoes the experience of pain, for example. We say, "I see such-and-such" and "I hear such-and-such," and we constantly use the first-person pronoun in our speech. There is no disputing the existence of the conventional level of "self" that we all experience in our day-to-day life.

Questions arise, however, when we try to understand what that "self" or "I" really is. In probing these questions we may try to extend the analysis beyond day-to-day life—we may, for example, recollect ourselves in our youth. When you recollect something from your youth, you have a close sense of identification with the state of the body and your sense of self at that age. When you were young, there was a self. As you get older there is a self. There is also a self that pervades both stages. An individual can recollect his or her experiences of youth, his or her experiences of old age, and so on. We identify with our bodily states and sense of self, our "I" consciousness.

Many philosophers and, particularly, religious thinkers have sought to understand the nature of the individual, that "self" or "I," that maintains this continuity over time. This has been especially important within the Indian tradition. The non-Buddhist Indian schools talk about *atman,* which is roughly translated as "self" or "soul"; and in other non-Indian religious traditions, such as Christianity and Judaism, we hear discussion about the "soul" of a being.

In the Indian context, *atman* has the distinct meaning of an agent that is independent of the living and breathing individual. In the Hindu tradition, for example, there is a belief in reincarnation, which has inspired a lot of debate. I have also found references to certain forms of mystical practice in which a consciousness or soul assumes the body of a newly dead person. In order to make sense of a soul assuming another body, we would need to posit some kind of agent that is independent of the observable elements of the individual. On the whole, non-Buddhist Indian schools have more or less come to the conclusion that *self* refers to this independent agent, to something that is independent of our body and mind. Buddhist traditions, on the other hand, have rejected the temptation to posit a "self," an atman, or a soul that is independent of our body and mind.

Among Buddhist schools the consensus is that "self" or "I" must be understood solely in terms of the body and mind. But as to what, exactly, we refer when we say "I" or "self," there has been divergence of opinion even among Buddhist thinkers. Many Buddhist schools maintain that in the final analysis we must identify the self with the consciousness of the person. Through analysis, we can show how our body is a kind of contingent fact, and that what continues across time is really a being's consciousness.

Of course, other Buddhist thinkers have rejected the move to identify self with consciousness, resisting the urge to seek some kind of eternal, abiding, or enduring self. Such thinkers have argued that following that kind of reasoning is, in a sense, succumbing to the ingrained need to grasp at something. An analysis of the nature of self along these lines will yield nothing, because the quest involved here is not scientific but metaphysical; for in the quest for a metaphysical self, we are going beyond the domain of everyday language and everyday experience. Therefore "self," "person," and "agent" must be understood purely in terms of how we experience our sense of self. We should not go beyond the level of the conventional understanding of self and person. We should develop an understanding of our existence in terms of our bodily and mental existence so that "self" and "person" are in some sense understood as designations wholly dependent upon mind and body.

Chandrakirti used the example of a chariot in his *Guide to the*

Middle Way. When you subject the concept of *chariot* to analysis, you are never going to find some kind of metaphysically or substantially real chariot that is independent of the parts of the chariot. But this does not mean the chariot doesn't exist. Similarly, when we subject "self" to such analysis, we cannot find a self independent of the mind and body that constitutes the existence of the individual.

This understanding of the self as arising interdependently must also extend to our understanding of other sentient beings. We designate "sentient beings" in dependence upon their constituent body and mind, what Buddhists call their *aggregates*.

> 2   Wherever I go, with whomever I go,
>   may I see myself as lower than all others, and
>   from the depth of my heart
>   may I consider them supremely precious.

The first verse pointed to the need to cultivate the thought of regarding all other sentient beings as precious. In the second verse, the point being made is that the recognition of the preciousness of other sentient beings, and the sense of caring that you develop on that basis, should not be grounded on a feeling of pity toward other sentient beings, that is, on the thought that they are inferior. Rather, what is being emphasized is a sense of caring for other sentient beings and a recognition of their preciousness, based on reverence and respect, as superior to us.

Moving on to another line of the verse, I think it is important to understand the expression "May I see myself as lower than all others" in the right context. Certainly it is not saying that you should engage in thoughts that would lead to lower self-esteem, or that you should lose all sense of hope and feel dejected, thinking, "I'm the lowest of all. I have no capacity, I cannot do anything and have no power." This is not the kind of consideration of lowness that is being referred to here.

Regarding oneself as lower than others has to be understood in relative terms. In certain ways, human beings can be regarded as superior to animals. We are equipped with the ability to judge between right and wrong and to think about the future. However, you could also argue that in other respects human beings are inferior to animals. For example, animals might not have the ability to judge between right and wrong in a moral sense, and they might not have the ability to see the long-term consequences of their actions, but within the animal realm there is a certain sense of order. If you look at the African savanna, you will see that predators prey on other animals only out of necessity when they are hungry. When they are not hungry, you can see them coexisting quite peacefully. But we human beings, despite our ability to judge between right and wrong, sometimes act out of pure greed. Sometimes we engage in actions purely out of indulgence—we kill out of a sense of sport, say, when we go hunting or fishing. So, in a sense, one could argue that human beings have proven to be *inferior* to animals. It is in such relative terms that we can regard ourselves as lower than others.

One of the reasons for using the word *lower* is to emphasize that normally when we give in to ordinary emotions of anger, hatred, strong attachment, and greed, we do so without any sense of restraint. Often we are totally oblivious to the impact our behavior has on other sentient beings. But by deliberately cultivating the thought of regarding others as superior and worthy of reverence, you provide yourself with a basis for restraint. Then, when emotions arise, they will not be so powerful that they can cause you to disregard the impact of your actions upon others. It is on these grounds that recognizing others as superior to yourself is suggested.

> 3   May I examine my mind in all actions
>   and as soon as a negative state occurs,
>   since it endangers myself and others,
>   may I firmly face and avert it.

This verse gets to the heart of what could be called the essence of the practice of the Buddhadharma. When we talk about Dharma in the context of Buddhism, we are talking about the cessation of suffering, or nirvana—the true Dharma. There are many levels of cessation; for example, restraint from murder could be Dharma. But this cannot be called Buddhist Dharma specifically because restraint from killing is something that even someone who is nonreligious can adopt as a result of obeying the law.

The essence of the Dharma in the Buddhist tradition is the state of freedom from suffering and from the defilements that lie at the root of suffering. This verse addresses how to combat these defilements, these afflictive emotions and thoughts. For a Buddhist practitioner, the real enemy is this enemy within. It is these emotional and mental afflictions that give rise to pain and suffering. The real task of a practitioner of Buddhadharma is to defeat this inner enemy

Since applying antidotes to these mental and emotional defilements lies at the heart of Dharma practice and is in some sense its foundation, the third verse suggests that it is very important to cultivate mindfulness right from the beginning. If you let negative emotions and thoughts arise inside you without any restraint, without any mindfulness of their negativity, then you are giving them free rein, and they can then develop to the point where there is no way to counter them. However, if you develop mindfulness of their negativity, then when they occur you will be able to stamp them out as soon as they arise. You will not give them the opportunity or the space to develop into full-blown negative emotional thoughts.

The verse suggests that we apply an antidote at the level of the felt experience. Instead of getting at the root of all emotion, the text suggests antidotes to specific negative emotions and thoughts. For example, to counter anger, you should cultivate love and compassion. To counter strong attachment to an object, you should cultivate thoughts about the impurity of that object, its undesirable nature, and so on. To counter your arrogance or pride, you need to reflect upon your shortcomings in order to give rise to a sense of humility. You can, for example, think about all the things in the world about which you are completely ignorant. Take sign language interpreters for the deaf: when I look at them and see the complex gestures with which they perform translations, I haven't a clue what is going on, and to see that is quite a humbling experience. From my own personal experience, whenever I have a little tingling sense of pride, I think of computers. It really calms me down!

> 4   When I see beings of a negative disposition
>   or those oppressed by negativity or pain,
>   may I, as if finding a treasure, consider them precious
>   for they are rarely met.

The reason beings of negative disposition are identified separately as a focus of training one's mind is because when you encounter such people, you may give in to the temptation to react in some strong negative way. In a sense, such beings pose a greater challenge to your ability to maintain your basic training, and hence they merit our special attention.

You can then go on to apply this sentiment to society in general. Among ordinary people there is a temptation or tendency to reject certain groups of people, to marginalize them and to not want to embrace them within the wider fold of the community. People who are branded as criminals are an example. In these cases, it is even more important for the practitioner to make an extra effort to try to embrace them so that they may be given a second chance in society and also an opportunity to restore their sense of self esteem. Similarly, there is also within society the temptation to ignore or deny the existence of incurable illnesses, such as AIDS, when one thinks, "That will never happen to me." There is a tendency to turn a blind eye to these things. In these cases too, a true practitioner should consciously reflect upon such phenomena and try to face them. One should cultivate one's mind so that one can empathize and relate to them.

5   Whenever others, out of jealousy,
      revile and treat me in other unjust ways,
      may I accept this defeat myself
      and offer the victory to others.

From a conventional legal point of view, if allegations are made against someone unjustly with no grounds or basis, we feel justified in reacting with anger and a sense of injustice. For a Buddhist practitioner, however, it is recommended that you not react this way, especially if the consequence of that unjust treatment is that you alone and no one else is hurt. A true practitioner of mind training is encouraged to accept defeat and offer victory, averting an outburst of outrage and anger.

> 6   When someone whom I have helped
>   or in whom I have placed great hope
>   harms me with great injustice,
>   may I see that one as a sacred friend.

Usually when we help someone, we tend to expect something in return. When someone is close to us, we have certain expectations of that person. And if that person, instead of responding to us in a positive way and repaying our kindness, inflicts harm upon us, we normally feel a sense of outrage. Our sense of disappointment and hurt are so strong and so deep that we feel that we are entirely justified in reacting with outrage and anger. For a true practitioner it is suggested that you not give in to that kind of normal response but rather utilize the opportunity for training, as a lesson and a teaching. The practitioner should regard that person as a true teacher of patience, for it is in situations like this that the training of patience is most needed. One should acknowledge the value of that person as a rare, precious teacher instead of reacting with anger and hostility.

This is not to suggest, however, that a true practitioner should simply yield to whatever harm or injustice is being inflicted upon him or her. In fact, according to the precepts of the bodhisattva, one should respond to injustice with a strong countermeasure, especially if there is any danger that the perpetrator of the crime is going to continue negative actions in the future or if other sentient beings are adversely affected. What is required is sensitivity to context. If a particular injustice happens and brings no wider consequences to bear upon either the perpetrator of the crime or upon other sentient beings, then perhaps you should let it pass.

7   In short, may I offer both directly and indirectly
     all joy and benefit to all beings, my mothers,
     and may I myself
     secretly take on all of their hurt and suffering.

In this verse the compassion referred to is so strong that, at least at the level of thought, one is willing take upon oneself all the suffering, pain, and hurt of all beings and to take on the negativities that lie at the root of these sufferings. One can also share all the positive qualities one has, such as one's joy, the causes of joy, roots of virtue, positive actions, and so on. One offers these positive qualities to other sentient beings.

The adverb *secretly* refers to the *tonglen* practice, the practice of giving and taking—taking on the suffering of others and offering them our joy and virtue. As the word *secretly* suggests, it is a form of practice that may not be suitable at the beginning stage, for it requires a certain depth of courage and commitment. In terms of the actual practice of giving and taking, tonglen practice is done in conjunction with the process of breathing—exhaling and inhaling.

The word *secretly* may also indicate the need for integrity on the part of the practitioner so that the practice of tonglen is done in a discreet way and the practitioner does not become an exhibitionist. A true practitioner must cultivate a spiritual training such as tonglen discreetly. The Kadampa master Geshe Chekawa states in his *Seven-Point Training of the Mind,* "Our inner states of mind and thoughts and emotions need to be radically transformed and overhauled, but our external appearance should remain the same." The point here is that it is dangerous for practitioners to succumb to the temptation to show off. Sometimes what happens, especially these days, is that people who have only a little experience may assume an air of importance or spirituality, which only cheapens one's true experience. Genuine practice of mind training requires humility and integrity.

The reference to all beings here as "my mothers" suggests the practice of holding all beings to be as dear as our own mother. In the Buddhist teachings on rebirth, in fact, all beings are said to have been our mother in a past life—giving birth to us, feeding us, and keeping us from harm—and we should recall that kindness, even when someone currently appears to us as harmful.

8   May they not be defiled by the concepts
       of the eight mundane concerns
       and, aware that all things are illusory,
       may they, ungrasping, be free from bondage.

The first two lines of this verse emphasize the need to ensure that spiritual practice and mind training are not polluted by worldly concerns such as fame, wealth, and pleasure. This is important even for a spiritual teacher. For example, when I sit on the throne and give a lecture, if somewhere in my thoughts there is a sense of curiosity—"Have I performed well?" "What do people think of my lecture?" "Are they happy with it?" "Will they praise me?"—this will pollute the spiritual training. These mundane concerns should not obscure and pollute true spiritual training.

The last two lines of this verse stress the need to situate mind training within a full understanding of ultimate truth, of emptiness. These lines state that you should develop the awareness that all things are illusory and, without grasping, free yourself from bondage. But before you can understand everything in terms of its illusory nature, you first need to negate the substantial reality of everything, including your own "self." There is no possibility of perceiving the illusory nature of everything unless you first negate the substantial reality of existence.

How do we develop this understanding? It is not enough simply to imagine that everything is empty and devoid of substantial existence or to simply repeat this verse in one's mind, like a formula. What is required is a genuine insight into emptiness through a rational process of analysis and reflection.

One of the most effective and convincing ways to understand how everything lacks a substantial reality is to understand interdependence, the dependent origination of everything. What is unique about the understanding of dependent origination is that it provides us with the possibility of finding that middle way between total nothingness on the one hand and substantial or independent existence on the other. The understanding that things are interdependent and dependently originated in itself suggests that things lack independent existence. And the idea that things originate in relation to others through a complex matrix of dependently originating elements also protects you from the danger of falling into the opposite view of nihilism—thinking that nothing exists. So by finding that true middle way, you can arrive at a genuine understanding and insight into emptiness.

Once you find this kind of insight in your meditation, when you interact with the world, with the people and objects around you, there is a new quality to your engagement with the world that arises out of your awareness of the illusory nature of reality. This new way of engaging in the world gives us a certain freedom from narrow concerns and allows us to work more steadily for the well-being of others. As such, it is a powerful basis for living the compassionate life.

Generating the Mind of Enlightenment

W E HAVE SPOKEN about the nature of compassion and the procedure for training one's mind and cultivating compassion. The special verses below are recited for the purpose of generating bodhichitta, the wish to free all sentient beings from suffering. When reciting the verses, you should try to recollect your full understanding of compassion and the need for cultivating it.

The first verse is a formal taking of refuge. Those of you who are practicing Buddhists, take refuge here. Non-Buddhist religious practitioners—Christians, Jews, Muslims, and others—can take refuge in your own religion's deity and use that formula as a way of reaffirming your faith in that deity.

The second verse pertains to the generation of the mind of enlightenment. The third verse really gives us a sense of courage and also a sense of inspiration that help us sustain our commitment to the altruistic principles. As you recite these verses, you should reflect upon their meaning and cultivate the right contemplation in your mind.

I think these three verses are very powerful. If you agree and feel comfortable with them, you should think about and recite these verses whenever you have the time. It will give you some inner strength, and this is very valuable.

> With a wish to free all beings
> I shall always go for refuge
> to the Buddha, Dharma, and Sangha,
> until I reach full enlightenment.

> Enthused by wisdom and compassion
> today in the Buddha's presence
> I generate the mind for full awakening
> for the benefit of all sentient beings.

> As long as space remains,
> as long as sentient beings remain,
> until then, may I too remain
> and dispel the miseries of the world.

Index

Suggested Further Reading

By the Dalai Lama

THE GOOD HEART

A Buddhist Perspective on the Teachings of Jesus

224 pages, 0-86171-138-6, $14.95

"Arguably the best book on inter-religious dialogue published to date. One does not say such things lightly, but in a very real sense this is a holy book."—Huston Smith, author of *The Illustrated World's Religions*

THE WORLD OF TIBETAN BUDDHISM

An Overview of Its Philosophy and Practice

Translated and edited by Geshe Thupten Jinpa

224 pages, 0-86171-097-5, $15.95

"The definitive book on Tibetan Buddhism by the world's ultimate authority."—*The Reader's Review*

"The perfect introduction for Westerners."—*Small Press*

THE MEANING OF LIFE

Buddhist Perspectives on Cause and Effect

164 pages, 0-86171-173-4, $15.95

"The Dalai Lama's kindness and wit make this journey into the inner psychic environment highly accessible. His Holiness presents the basic world view of Buddhism while answering some of life's most profound and challenging questions." —*Branches of Light*

"The Dalai Lama's responses to questions convey a sense of his personal warmth and compassion." —*CHOICE*

"Studded with jewels." —*Shambhala Sun*

IMAGINE ALL THE PEOPLE

The Dalai Lama with Fabien Ouaki

192 pages, 0-86171-150-5, $14.95

If you could sit down with the Dalai Lama and talk about anything, what would you discuss? Here, in spontaneous, lively discussion, the Dalai Lama holds forth on money, politics, and life as it could be.

MINDSCIENCE

An East-West Dialogue

The Dalai Lama and others.

152 pages, 0-86171-066-5, $14.95

Robert A.F. Thurman, Daniel Goleman, and authorities from the fields of psychiatry, psychology, neuroscience, and education join His Holiness for an explorative, historic dialogue between modern science and Buddhism.

"Slender but comprehensive...cuts right to the core issues of its compelling topic."—*The Quest*

"Lively and interesting...full of pearls."—*Shambhala Sun*

KALACHAKRA TANTRA

Rite of Initiation

Translated by Jeffrey Hopkins

512 pages, 0-86171-151-3, $22.95

Of the hundreds of tantras, Kalachakra is the among the most important. Here, the Dalai Lama presents the series of initiations for the generation stage of this tantra, interspersed with his commentary. Eminent scholar Jeffrey Hopkins provides a comprehensive introduction to the symbolism and history behind the practice.

OPENING THE EYE OF NEW AWARENESS

160 pages, 0-86171-155-6, $14.95

"All of His Holiness' many publications are in some sense commentaries on this first book. A clear and concise exposition of the essentials of Buddhist thought."—from the Introduction by Donald Lopez, Jr.

SLEEPING, DREAMING, AND DYING

An Exploration of Consciousness

264 pages, 0-86171-123-8, $16.95

"Intelligent, insightful. Anyone interested in psychology, neuroscience, or the alternative worlds of dreams and the afterlife will surely enjoy the discoveries contained within."—*NAPRA ReView*

WISDOM PUBLICATIONS
Publisher of Buddhist Books. For everyone.
199 Elm Street, Somerville, MA 02144 USA
wisdompubs.org ∾ 800.272.4050

Distributed to the trade by: National Book Network (NBN)
Ph: 800.462.6420 ∾ Fax: 800.338.4550

About Wisdom

Wisdom Publications, a nonprofit publisher, is dedicated to making available authentic Buddhist works for the benefit of all. We publish translations of the sutras and tantras, commentaries and teachings of past and contemporary Buddhist masters, and original works by the world's leading Buddhist scholars. We publish our titles with the appreciation of Buddhism as a living philosophy and with the special commitment to preserve and transmit important works from all the major Buddhist traditions.

If you would like to learn more about Wisdom, or to browse our books online, visit our website at wisdompubs.org.

If you would like to order a copy of our mail-order catalog, please contact us at:

Wisdom Publications
199 Elm Street
Somerville, Massachusetts 02144 USA
Telephone: (617) 776-7416 • Fax: (617) 776-7841
Email: sales@wisdompubs.org • www.wisdompubs.org

Wisdom Publications is a nonprofit, charitable 501(c)(3) organization affiliated with the Foundation for the Preservation of the Mahayana Tradition (FPMT).